Birds
of Field & Forest

A TIME-LIFE TELEVISION BOOK

Editor: Eleanor Graves
Series Editor: Charles Osborne
Text Editor: Richard Oulahan
　　Associate Text Editor: Bonnie Johnson
　　Author: Peter Wood
　　Assistant Editor: Peter Ainslie
　　Writer: Don Earnest
　　Literary Research: Ellen Schachter
　　Text Research: Constance R. Roosevelt
　　Copy Editors: Robert J. Myer, Greg Weed
Picture Editor: Richard O. Pollard
　　Picture Research: Judith Greene
　　Permissions: Cecilia Waters
Book Designer and Art Director: Jos. Trautwein
　　Art Assistant: Carl Van Brunt
Production Coordinator: Jane L. Quinson

WILD, WILD WORLD OF ANIMALS
TELEVISION PROGRAM
Producers: Jonathan Donald and Lothar Wolff
This Time-Life Television Book is published by Time-Life Films, Inc.
Bruce L. Paisner, *President*
J. Nicoll Durrie, *Business Manager*

THE AUTHOR

PETER WOOD worked for a decade on the Time-Life Books nature series and wrote two books for the American Wilderness series: *Caribbean Isles* and *Sierra Madre*. Currently a free-lance writer, he lives in Newport, Rhode Island.

THE CONSULTANT

BERTEL BRUUN, a practicing neurologist in New York City, has studied birds since his childhood. He was co-author of the widely used *Field Guide to Birds of North America* and author of the prestigious *Birds of Europe* as well as other books and scientific articles on birds. He has traveled widely in pursuit of his interest. He is a member of the American Ornithologists' Union and a member of the board of the Holy Land Conservation Fund.

Birds
of Field & Forest

Based on the television series
Wild, Wild World of Animals

Published by
TIME-LIFE FILMS

The excerpt and illustration from "My Senegalese Birds and Siamese Cats,"
by James Thurber, is reprinted from Lanterns and Lances, copyright
© 1960 by James Thurber, by permission of Harper & Row and Hamish
Hamilton Ltd.

ISBN 0-913948-13-6

Library of Congress Catalog Card Number: 77-5596

Contents

Introduction
by Peter Wood

Sandhill crane

Stroll through field or forest on a spring morning and it is hard to believe that the golden age of birds is past. Yet ten million years ago, during the Pliocene epoch, there were roughly three times as many different kinds of birds as there are living today. In filling ecological niches left vacant by a great and mysterious dying of dinosaurs and other ancient reptiles, the birds literally flew off to a fast start. Their feathered mobility gave them an early advantage over their only warm-blooded competition, the mammals. Ornithologists estimate that there are still roughly 9,000 species of birds, compared with 15,000 species of mammals and 20,000 of fishes.

Taxonomists assign the surviving birds to 27 orders—the parrots, the owls, the loons, and so forth. Of these, 18 orders, many of them represented in this book, may be arbitrarily grouped under the broad heading of field and forest, nonperching birds. They are as diverse as the habitats in which they are found, ranging from mountain meadows to jungle thickets.

Spectacular in their own right, eight orders are represented mainly by water birds, which are pictured in another volume in this series. The remaining order, which consists of the perching birds, called the Passeriformes, contains about three-fifths of the world's birds, and range in size from 36-inch lyre birds to the three-inch African crombecs and include most common varieties of birds—and many more not at all common. Evolutionary newcomers on the family tree of birds, and highly capable of adapting to change, the Passeriformes warrant a volume of their own.

Compared to most perching birds, those of field and forest have suffered greatly at the hands of man, who has been a highly effective exterminator. But he has also regarded them always with admiration and awe. Their courtship behavior, for instance, tempts the observer to credit them with artistry. The exquisite tracery of a single peacock feather seems far more than enough to achieve its practical purpose—to catch a peahen's eye—and the quill-rattling flourishes that accompany the display of a hundred eyes in the peacock's nuptial fan appear extravagant to the point of luxury. No wonder that natives around the world wear the feathers and imitate in dance the antics of some of their local birds. The Blackfoot Indians of the American Northwest mimic the foot-stamping, bowing and strutting of the sage grouse. New Guinea natives revere the ungainly hornbill for its domesticity in nesting and the nurturing of young. There is good reason for birds to strike so sympathetic a chord in man. Despite enormously dissimilar appearances, humans and birds share several telling biological traits. Both are "eye" animals, experiencing the world on much the same terms—at a distance and through the primary senses of sight and sound, rather than the more intimate senses of taste, touch and smell. Man's eyesight is excellent. He can see long distances and is one of the few mammals that are able to discern color

A dense deciduous forest, a steep rocky bluff and a meandering stream provide an ideal, protected sanctuary for woodland birds in the Ozark Mountains of Arkansas and southern Missouri.

Dodo, 1680

Lord Howe Island parrot, 1869

Tahiti parakeet, circa 1850

New Caledonia lorikeet, circa 1860

Like a gallery of ghosts bearing silent witness, the birds illustrated on these pages, with the dates of their extinction, have all been exterminated by man. The wingless dodo has become the symbol of relentless man-made extinction: Less than a century after Dutch sailors discovered the big birds, the last dodo was dead. The passenger pigeon was hunted down on a scale unmatched by any human genocide. Whatever the reason for their extinction, one melancholy fact is certain: More and more bird species are vanishing from the earth, and with each passing decade the pace of extermination grows faster.

Birds do all that and do it better. Vultures soaring a mile high can locate buried carrion by spotting insects buzzing above the spot. The night vision of owls has been shown to be more than 10 times as sensitive as man's. The curious jerky gait of pigeons and chickens sharpens their view of the world: It is difficult to focus when the head is moving, particularly in viewing objects close by. So, like pirouetting ballet dancers, they hold their heads stationary while their bodies move, then they snap their necks forward to catch up. Another feature of the eyes of birds is that, like certain reptiles, they are protected with three lids—bottom, top and a so-called nictitating membrane that sweeps across the eye from the side to keep it moist and to guard it against foreign objects.

Sound and hearing are as essential to birds as they are to man for communications, navigation and food-gathering. To keep in touch, birds call and sing, each with a distinctive sound that proclaims its individuality. The oilbird of South America and certain swiftlets from East Asia, both of which roost in caves, are able to navigate safely in total darkness by echo-ranging like bats. The barn owl catches mice by homing on the faint noise they make scurrying through the grass.

Humans also share their mode of walking with most birds. Both stand on

Brown-headed parrot, 1773–74

Cuban red macaw, 1885

Carolina parakeet, 1914

Passenger pigeon, 1914

Heath hen, 1932

their hind feet. Bipedalism frees the upper limbs—in man for tool-using, in birds for flight. As it has turned out, the ability to use tools was an evolutionary turning point. Along with language, it rapidly elevated man into a category above all other animals. But two to four million years ago a visitor from outer space weighing the future prospects of the various animal classes might well have backed the birds. At that time man was still a relatively rare and unimportant animal. By contrast, birds had already populated much of the world and adapted to nearly every environment. This extraordinary radiation was made possible by the capacity for flight, coupled with warm-bloodedness and adaptability—attributes that opened up worlds inaccessible to other earthbound creatures.

An important advantage of flight is recognized in the secondary dictionary definition of the verb "to fly": to escape, to flee. Few defensive mechanisms can match it. Where birds have been most vulnerable is in the earthbound nest. There, to protect their flightless young, they have developed stealth, camouflage, the choice of inaccessible nesting sites, even the feigning of a broken wing to lure off predators.

Apart from its value as an escape mechanism, flight proved a bonanza as a means of food-gathering. It extended the foraging range and opened up larders largely closed to earthbound vertebrates—the rich diet provided by flying insects, along with fruits, berries and flowers that grow on high bushes and trees. And if the destruction by certain birds of some food crops has branded them as pests, it should be remembered that without birds to eat them and keep them in check, insects might overwhelm the world and leave it virtually uninhabitable by man.

Paul Singer

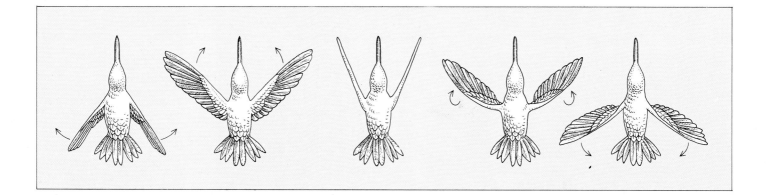

The hummingbird is the only bird capable of flying in any direction. A more amazing feat, however, is its ability to hover in the air, illustrated above. In the upward stroke the wing moves with the upper edge forward. As it comes down, however, the wing is rotated almost 180 degrees so the upper edge faces downward. Both motions produce lift without any movement of the body forward or backward and have the effect of suspending the bird in the air.

Flight also permitted rapid travel across great distances, enabling birds to migrate and exploit the seasonally abundant Arctic and alpine regions. Migratory birds could fly there prior to the brief summer, raise their young in the midst of plenty and the safety of relative isolation and then fly to warmer climates before winter closed in. Even hummingbirds take advantage of such opportunities—particularly the ruby-throated species, which travels 2,000 miles between its winter and summer habitats. The long flights of some hummingbirds are especially striking feats; because of their diminutive size, they need a steady diet of high-energy food, usually nectar, to maintain their metabolic rate. To accumulate energy comparable to that expended by a hummingbird, a 170-pound man would have to eat 285 pounds of hamburger in one day or consume double his weight in potatoes. At night in cool climates, when hummingbirds are not feeding, their temperatures may drop

Cross-country flight of the itinerant Rüppell's griffon vulture, is illustrated at right. The vulture gains altitude by hitching a ride on a thermal, a column of air that rises when heated by the sun-warmed earth. The bird flies upward in steady circles, staying close to the core of the air column, where the lift is greatest, then glides for a distance, looking for carrion as it descends. If no food is sighted, the bird catches another thermal to continue its search.

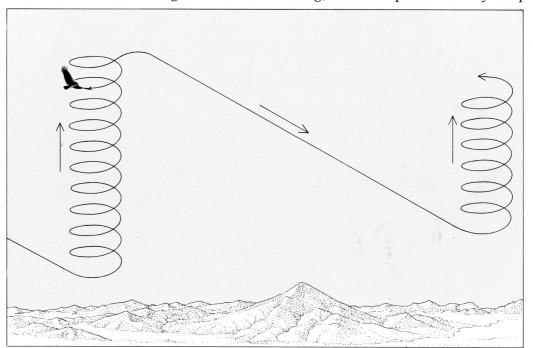

as much as 20 degrees Farenheit, and they enter an energy-saving state of semitorpor similar to hibernation.

In turning their forelimbs to flight, birds adapted them to highly differentiated modes of life—long, tapering wings for swifts that capture insects in midair; huge saillike wings for soaring vultures; intricately hinged wings for hovering hummingbirds. Two other major extremities were also modified for food-gathering: beaks and feet. Often the adaptation was highly specific—for instance, the downcurved needlelike beak of one hummingbird, the white-tipped sicklebill, which is adapted to fit the wild plantain flower, or the spurlike spines on the talons of fishing owls that enable them to grasp their slippery prey. As a general rule, large carnivorous birds developed powerful talons for clutching and hooked, serrated beaks for tearing flesh. Nightjars and other insect-eaters that hunt on the fly evolved wide gaping mouths, the better to scoop up their swarming food. Others, like the bee-eaters, grew tweezer-shaped beaks, good for snapping up insects one at a time. Strong feet helped the omnivorous gallinaceous birds that scratch a living from the ground. Seed- and nut-eaters have evolved with beaks especially suited for cracking hulls. Carried beyond a certain point, however, specialization has become a synonym for vulnerability. North America's largest woodpecker, the ivory-billed of the Southeast, was exquisitely built to feed on certain wood-boring insects that infested dead and dying trees of advanced age. As the virgin forest disappears, they approach extinction.

The list of similar avian disappearances—which include the dodo, the passenger pigeon and the heath hen—runs to more than 80 in the past 300 years. Species come and species go in the natural course of evolution, but not at that terrible pace. The majority of the species extinctions have been island birds with no tolerance at all for man and the predatory animals that accompany him, such as rats and cats. And as man levels and invades more and more of the world's wild regions, many more incredibly beautiful creatures will almost inevitably vanish.

Many of these somber events may be delayed with sound conservation measures, but many probably cannot be put off forever. Yet one thing is certain: Birds will survive, for the very same specialization that dooms certain of them as species is a measure of the adaptability of the class as a whole. Pheasants gleaning a living in Iowa cornfields, for example, are hybrids of stock native to the Old World. Man brought them to the New World after keeping their ancestors for hundreds of generations in Europe. Today, brilliant in their ancient Asian plumage, the birds thrive in their new habitat.

Pheasants and Peacocks

"The peacock . . . spreads his fan-like tail coverts and approaches the female obliquely with the drab rear-side of his fan exposed to her." So American ornithologist J. C. Welty describes the cautious beginning of one of nature's most impressive courtship displays. Then, Welty continues, "At just the right distance, he suddenly swings himself around and dazzles her with every one of the hundred or more shimmering 'eyes' vibrating and every quill rattling. To climax the performance, he screams with demonic ardor and then settles back to let his theatrics sink in." Almost invariably the "eyes" have it, and the peahen succumbs to the overwhelming invitation.

Yet the extravagant plumage that makes this stirring performance such a conspicuous triumph for the peacock also carries an exorbitant price tag: vulnerability to predators. "How much easier the life of a wild peacock would be," speculated the American ornithologist William Beebe, "if he could dispense with his train and his iridescence." Beebe's remark could apply equally to pheasants, among which are some of the world's most gorgeously adorned birds. For the fine feathers are more than just the accouterments of courtship; they are exclusively male equipment that serve to divert the attention of the natural enemies of the birds, including two-legged hunters with guns, away from the drab-feathered females and chicks.

Pheasants and peacocks are gallinaceous fowls, and, like the best known of their breed, the domesticated chicken, they are plump birds that scratch a living from the ground with powerful claws and omnivorous appetites. There is very little that gallinaceous birds will not eat: seeds, berries, nuts, grubs, snails, grasshoppers—even, on occasion, grit to aid the digestion. They prefer to walk. But they are capable of flight, in sudden, furious flutters interspersed with long glides, to find safe roosts high in the trees at night or to escape from earthbound predators. And Galliformes must reckon with plenty of enemies, for their succulent flesh is as highly esteemed by four-legged and winged predators as it is by man. In the early part of this century Beebe, a noted authority on pheasants, saw a great deal of slaughter in the course of a 17-month odyssey through Asia and the East Indies, the native habitat of most of these dazzling birds. His first sight of a rare monal pheasant, which he described as one of "the most brilliantly iridescent birds in the world," was the talon-ripped body of a cock he found high on a windy Himalayan mountainside

in eastern Nepal. In all, Beebe observed and catalogued nearly 80 pheasant species. His sightings include the great argus of Indochina and Malaysia; the golden from the highlands of China, which many ornithologists consider the most beautiful of the family; and the Lady Amherst of Tibet, China and Burma. The latter is a stunner, with white, green, blue and red raiment etched in black and trailing tail feathers 46 inches long.

The kinship of these fashion plates with the handsomely plumed ring-necked pheasant, which has been successfully introduced into Europe and North America and has become one of the most common American game birds, is obvious. Besides tracking down pheasants and peacocks in their native climes, William Beebe sought out another close relative, notable as the bird that has made the greatest impact on man, the red jungle fowl. Originally from Southeast Asia, it was the ancestor of every one of the vast variety of domestic breeds of chickens in the world—and with its scarlet coxcomb and wattles, the red jungle fowl has an obvious family connection with every leghorn or Rhode Island red rooster that ever lorded it over a barnyard.

Pheasants and some of their kin have been domesticated, or at least semidomesticated, for thousands of years— longer than any other birds, even though they come from some of the world's most remote corners. The Lady Amherst has been seen at 15,000 feet in the Himalayas, the silver pheasant at 9,000 feet in the dripping mountain forests of Burma. Chickens were first domesticated by Bronze Age people over 4,000 years ago—first for cockfighting, later for their meat and eggs. Peacocks strutted and posed in Egyptian aviaries. About 1,000 B.C. King Solomon, according to the Bible, imported peafowl to adorn his gardens. No zoo today is complete without its resident peacock. Part of this adaptability to domestication lies in hardiness. It is not by chance that the ring-necked pheasant—now a hybridized descendant of several Old World species—has proliferated in American farmlands from Maine to California and as far south as Kansas since its first successful introduction in 1882.

The ring-neck's survival in North America owes much to the fact that man's laws follow the laws of nature. In most states only cock pheasants are legally fair game. And fortunately for the family's survival, the males are expendable. There are usually more than enough proud cock pheasants to keep the population healthily stable.

14

Popular Game Bird

The ring-necked pheasant, the most common of the wild fowl, is a big, handsome bird that was originally a native of the Orient, found from Asia Minor to China and Korea. Its popularity as a game bird, however, led to its becoming widespread throughout Europe by the 18th century and later in Hawaii, New Zealand and North America.

Among the 34 subspecies of ring-necks some, like the one below, have been so thoroughly hybridized that they completely lack the white collar for which the group is named. They grow to a length of up to three feet and feed on seeds, plants and insects. During the spring breeding season males establish harems. They woo the females by extending their wings (right) and circling the hens, showing off their splendid plumage. Each hen lays eight to 15 eggs for which she becomes solely responsible, since the cocks depart after mating to live a solitary life until the next breeding season.

A dark-necked form of the ring-necked pheasant peers through underbrush (above). This subspecies was first introduced into the eastern United States from England late in the 18th century but is now rare in America. Conversely, the strutting white-collared variety (right), originally from China and Mongolia, has flourished since its arrival in Oregon in the 1880s.

Pheasant Finery

The most elegantly plumed of all game birds are the pheasants. The plump, long-legged birds are found throughout central Asia. Pheasants have short, rounded wings that swiftly carry them away from danger with short, rapid beats. Their aerial equipment is not suited for sustained flight, however, and pheasants take to the air only as a last resort, preferring to flee on foot instead. (The photograph at left, of an airborne Himalayan monal pheasant, the national bird of Nepal, is rare.)

Himalayan monals frequent open woodlands high in the mountains. When the cold and snow of winter arrive they retreat down the mountain to warmer zones. Snow presents no problem for the blood pheasant (below). Even in the dead of a Himalayan winter these birds survive in mountain passes at altitudes up to 9,000 feet by scratching out roots and seeds from under the snow.

The white-spotted, crimson plumage of the satyr tragopan (above) has made it a favorite zoo animal since 1863, when the first specimen was brought to the London Zoo from its native habitat in the central and eastern Himalayas. The flaxen crested golden pheasant (left) is another popular cage bird. But despite the fact that it has been depicted in Chinese art and literature for centuries, relatively little is known about its habits in the wild.

19

A Magnificent Train

There are many splendid courting rituals in the bird kingdom, including the mating dances of the whooping crane (pages 116–117) and the prairie chicken (page 28). But none is so visually breathtaking as the unfolding of the glittering feather train of the peacock. The photographs on the following pages show an albino and an Indian peacock in full display. The train is actually the peacock's upper tail coverts. These magnificent plumes, each of which is studded with multicolored ocelli (opposite), extend far beyond the bird's 20 drab tail feathers, which act as supports when the train is elevated. When not erect, as in the stately common peacock below, the train trails several feet behind the bird.

Peafowl are among the largest gallinaceous birds. In the wild they feed in grassy open spaces during the day and retreat to the branches of trees to roost in early evening. Peacock chicks begin practicing their display techniques at an early age, but it is not until they are three years old that their trains, which may be as long as five feet, reach full size.

Turkeys and Grouse

Despite a name that suggests an origin on the steppes of Anatolia, the turkey is a bird so symbolic of America that Benjamin Franklin seriously suggested it as the national symbol (page 44). The common turkey of North America and its rarer cousin, the ocellated turkey of the Central American lowlands (the word "ocellated," meaning eyelike, refers to the spots, like those of peacocks, on its feathers), are the sole members of the subfamily Meleagridinae. Discovered and exported by early Spanish explorers—the bird was first domesticated by the Aztecs—turkeys quickly took their place in European barnyards and later spread throughout Asia. They are called turkeys, according to one legend, because English cooks during the reign of Henry VIII got the American fowl mixed up with another exotic and tasty gallinaceous bird, the guineafowl of sub-Saharan Africa, to which the Turkish Empire was then the gateway.

In behavior, turkeys resemble pheasants and may have evolved from an early dispersal of pheasant relatives to America from Asia. Like pheasants, they roost in trees but spend their days foraging on the forest floor. They can fly strongly for short distances, flapping madly until they are airborne and then gliding to a heavy landing. Turkeys are polygamous, with a single tom belligerently ruling and defending his own territory and group of hens. John James Audubon described a battle between two toms, "their wings drooping, their tails partly raised, their body feathers ruffled and their heads covered with blood." His account is a reminder that these birds are wild creatures of a ferocity that no longer exists in the domestic breed: "If, as they thus struggle and gasp for breath, one of them should lose his hold, his chance is over, for the other, still holding fast, hits him violently with spurs and wings, and in a few minutes brings him to the ground. The moment he is dead the conqueror treads him under foot but what is strange, not with hatred but with all the motions which he employs in caressing the female."

Smaller than turkeys, but more esteemed as game birds because their bursts of rapid flight make them a special challenge for sportsmen, are the grouse. There are 16 species in this family, some polygamous, some monogamous. The biggest grouse is the capercaillie of northern Europe and Asia, nearly the size of a turkey and of much the same disposition. Heavily hunted, this magnificent black bird has become quite rare in most parts of Europe.

Among the smaller grouse are the three species of ptarmigans, two of which live close to the Arctic Circle; and true to their gallinaceous heritage, they do not migrate.

Given the lack of natural cover where they live, ptarmigans need every bit of camouflage they can muster. The rock ptarmigan is a master of the art. Snow white in winter, it molts to a mottled brown as the snow melts and is replaced by tundra grasses. To match the gray of its rocky surroundings, in the autumn it molts for a third time, one of the very few birds known to do so.

The largest North American grouse is the sage, with a range corresponding to that of sagebrush on the Western plains. Males weigh up to eight pounds and put on engaging displays of bowing and bobbing to attract females, motions that are imitated in the dances of plains Indians. Similar, though smaller, are the prairie chicken and sharp-tailed grouse. With a range stretching across the top two thirds of North America, the ruffed grouse is one of the New World's best-known native game birds. Though monogamous, it too goes through impressive come-hither mating antics each spring. Taking a stance on a hollow log—usually the same log season after season—it beats the air with cupped wings in an increasing tempo. The "drumming" sounds like distant thunder.

The most primitive gallinaceous bird is the hoatzin of the northeastern South American rain forest, whose peculiar appearance has persuaded some taxonomists to place it in an order all its own. With a crest of stiff feathers, a short beak and red eyes set in patches of naked blue skin, its small head and long neck have an ancient, prehistoric look.

Other turkey relatives are the megapodes, the "big feet," the only birds that incubate their eggs with other than body heat. There are a dozen species; the chicken-sized scrub fowl of the southwestern Pacific islands are typical. Scrub fowl use the heat of decaying vegetation to do their incubating. Standing on one foot and scratching vigorously backward with the other, they pile up litter in a very large mound; one has been measured that was 15 feet wide, 10 feet high and 60 feet long. When the pile has decomposed sufficiently to generate heat, the female excavates several chambers and lays an egg in each one. For the next two months the birds regulate the temperature to a constant 96° F. by adding or subtracting decaying vegetation. When the chicks finally hatch, they dig themselves out and go about their business without any more help from their parents.

Willow ptarmigan

The Tenacious Turkey

Since the first Thanksgiving in 1621, the turkey, now raised by the millions on turkey farms, has been the centerpiece of American holiday fare. The heavy-bodied, pheasantlike birds were so abundant in New England in pre-Revolutionary days that they sold for only a penny or two a pound. As men cleared the forest, the wild turkey disappeared from New England. With strict hunting laws and good game management, however, the birds have survived in the wild in other areas and are still abundant from Pennsylvania to Florida.

Turkeys are woodland inhabitants that spend their days foraging and their nights roosting in trees. During the winter months the males live in separate flocks from the hens and young. But with the onset of spring the toms begin their notable courting display. With red neck wattles distended and tail and wing feathers unfurled, they strut before the females, competing for their attention. The ritual continues for days until each male, like the one opposite, has assembled a group of as many as six hens with which to mate that season.

The business of gathering his harem over, a turkey and his hens forage for the acorns, insects, fruits and buds that make up their diet. Once she has mated, the hen goes off by herself to build a nest—usually a shallow depression dug out of the dense underbrush. The hen alone is responsible for incubating her eight to 15 eggs and for the care of her brood when they hatch some 28 days later.

Ritual Dancers of the Prairie

The prairie chicken cock (left) puts on one of the most elaborate shows in the animal kingdom when he performs his mating rite—an intricate dance that inspired the choreography for the ceremonies of the plains Indians. With tail and neck feathers held stiffly erect, head lowered in a deep bow and wings dropped, the cock dashes forward a few steps, stamps the ground and gracefully circles around several times. Then he fans his tail open and quickly snaps it shut. As he ends his dance, the brilliant air sacs on the sides of his neck puff up to the size of small oranges, and he sounds his love call—a loud, hollow noise that has given the whole ritual the name "booming."

The prairie chicken cock is not a solo performer. Each spring as many as 30 cocks gather at their traditional dancing ground, known as an "arena." At dawn and again at dusk, the booming of the chorus can be heard nearly a mile away. Another impressive dancer is the prairie chicken's cousin and fellow plainsman, the sage grouse (below).

Ardently trying to woo hens with their intricate courtship dances are a prairie chicken (left) and a sage grouse (above). During the mating season the display and booming also serve to defend the males' territory.

Rain-forest Primitives

For millions of years South America was an isolated land mass, and its lush tropical rain forests, with their bountiful food supply and unchanging warm climate, provided a rich habitat for the evolution and survival of some very distinctive species of birds. Among the strangest is the hoatzin (above), which bears a remarkably close resemblance to scientists' reconstructions of the primitive avian creature called *Archaeopteryx*.

Like that ancestor of birds, the hoatzin is not a good flier, able to do little more than glide from the branches of one shrubby tree to another a few hundred feet away. Chicks are born with claws on their wings, enabling them to clamber like quadrupeds through the trees. They also dive and swim to escape their enemies. Adults lose their wing claws and shun the water but develop peculiarities of their own, among them an enormous food-storage crop that also functions as a gizzard to prepare food for digestion, and eyelashes like those of mammals.

The curassow (opposite) is another jungle-dwelling tree glider with a primitive-looking physique, but this bird is far less exotic than it appears, being in fact a relative of the barnyard chicken.

30

A coif of curling feathered ringlets is the most striking physical feature of the curassow (below). Although this turkey-sized bird takes its name from the island of Curaçao in the Dutch West Indies, it has never been known to live there. In its natural range, from Mexico to northern South America, it has long been hunted for its succulent flesh and is now a threatened species.

Birds of Prey

Diurnal birds of prey—the Falconiformes—have stirred the imagination and admiration of man since the earliest times. Proud, fierce, strong and daring, these warriors of the sky are emblazoned on national arms and flags as symbols of patriotic pride and valor. Graven images of eagles were carried into battle with the Roman legions. Hooded, perched on the gloved fists of falconers, hawks and falcons have been hunting companions of man for centuries.

Not all predacious birds are Falconiformes—other birds, notably owls, are hunters, too—but all Falconiformes, or diurnal raptors, are classed as birds of prey. They are equipped with strong, downcurving beaks and powerful feet with opposable toes, tipped with deadly talons designed for grasping and hooking flesh. Their eyesight is exceptionally keen—many times sharper than man's—enabling them to spot prey from as much as a mile high in the sky, and their eyes have a piercing look that gives falcons and their kind an aggressive, haughty expression.

As strong, acrobatic fliers, though, it is their aggressive style that sets them apart from other birds. The archetypal falcon, the fearless peregrine, weighs only one or two pounds, but it will unhesitatingly attack much larger birds. Plummeting down in a classic power dive, or stoop—as falconers call it—which may reach speeds of up to 175 miles per hour, a peregrine can kill a four-pound barnacle goose. Attacking such relatively large quarry, the peregrine may not use its talons at all; it is likelier instead to smash the bird with its feet, stunning or crippling the prey in a midair explosion of feathers. The peregrine may let the dazed victim fall and then finish it off on the ground, severing its spinal column. Or it may execute a tight turn and seize the broken body in midair. Such skill and prowess have established the peregrine falcon above all others as the favorite bird for the ancient sport of falconry.

The largest group of the raptors are eagles, among which the archetype is the russet-crowned golden eagle of the wild mountain fastnesses in the northern hemisphere. With a wingspan that may reach seven feet, *Aquila*, as the golden eagle is called in Latin, was dubbed the king of birds and established as the symbol of imperial power by the Romans. Like many other countries, the United States chose an eagle—its own indigenous bald eagle—as its national symbol. With its snow-white head and imposing bulk it was considered an apt representation of national pride, though ornithologists—and Benjamin Franklin (page 44)—pointed out that the American eagle frequently eats carrion or steals prey rather than killing for itself.

Every raptor, from eagles to the smallest hawks, has wings that suit its particular mode of hunting. The forest hawks, such as the North American Cooper's hawk, have broad and relatively stubby wings, adapted to a hunting style that involves dashing among tree trunks and brush. Vultures and eagles, which soar at high altitudes, have longer, wider wings.

In general, vultures are exceptional as birds of prey. They are almost continually on the prowl—but generally let others do the killing. Some vultures have feet and beaks too weak to kill efficiently. In contrast to the awed esteem accorded most Falconiformes, vultures are disdained by man. Besides their hideous bare heads and their prevailing choice of diet, they squirt excrement over their own legs and feet. But their behavior is understandable. The digestive systems of vultures contain chemicals that kill the virulent bacteria that breed in the putrid meat they feed on. Their droppings are thought to contain the same disinfectants and to act as partial protection against contagion contracted by walking over rotting corpses. For the same reason vultures' heads are bare of feathers, permitting the sun's rays to disinfect those parts most likely to become covered with tainted blood.

In one respect, vultures command unreserved admiration. That is in their ability to fly or, more specifically, to soar. Two spectacular members of the family of New World vultures, the Andean and California condors (the latter, with a bare 50 or 60 surviving individuals, teeters on the knife edge of extinction), are among the largest flighted birds. Soaring, condors can stay aloft for hours on end with barely the flick of a wing tip.

The trick, as glider pilots have learned, is in riding thermal and wind-born updrafts. Without such flying aids, the big birds, such as the Rüppell's griffon vulture and the white-backed vultures of East Africa, would be virtually grounded. To get aloft each morning, vultures that live on the Serengeti Plain must wait until the heat of the sun begins to move the air. Once they are airborne, a mile high over their hunting grounds, their advantage is twofold. They are able to spot recent kills over a radius of many miles and, more importantly, locate other vultures heading toward a kill. Then, traveling at up to 50 miles per hour, they can beat the hyenas and other earthbound scavenging creatures to the spot and have a few minutes at the kill before being chased off by the bigger animals.

Turkey vultures

Hawks: Keen-eyed Predators

The hawk has a justly deserved reputation for ferocity and exhibits this tendency at an early age, as demonstrated by the nestling red-tailed hawk (opposite, top), rearing up to ward off an intruder. The defiant visage of the adult red-tail (above) displays two physical traits that translate this inborn spirit into a terrifying and deadly reality for its prey. One of these characteristics is the sharp cutting edge of the hooked upper mandible, which projects over the lower like a powerful pair of shears and can tear apart a stunned victim in a matter of minutes.

The other trait is the hawk's fabled eyesight, the keenest in the animal kingdom. Often as large as a man's, a hawk's eyes are so densely packed with nerve cells that it can spot a tiny mouse at great distances.

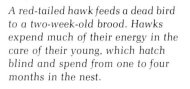

A red-tailed hawk feeds a dead bird to a two-week-old brood. Hawks expend much of their energy in the care of their young, which hatch blind and spend from one to four months in the nest.

Splendid Soarers

With broad, powerful wings rigidly curved, feet pulled back and head bent forward to eye the ground below, a hawk coming to earth is a majestic sight. The hawk is an aerodynamic marvel, able to maintain flight for long periods without exerting itself, completely motionless except for an occasional mild shrug to correct its course.

On the lookout for prey in the meadows and woodlands thousands of feet below, these accomplished aviators wheel in wide graceful circles as they ride on invisible columns of warm air rising up from the heated earth. During their spring and fall migrations, the paths that hawks most often choose are along mountain chains, where they can glide effortlessly for miles at a time on the updrafts that rise along the windward slopes. At one peak in Pennsylvania, appropriately named Hawk Mountain, the routes of so many of these gliding migrators converge that hundreds of hawkwatchers gather there each autumn to witness and photograph the spectacle.

The most abundant and widely distributed hawk in North America is the red-tailed hawk, shown here displaying its distinctive ruddy tail feathers. Although a graceful soarer, this large-bodied hawk moves with more deliberation than its slighter and more streamlined cousins.

Lethal Descent

Approaching the end of a rapid diving attack, or "stoop," a hawk, like the young one opposite, stiffens its legs and thrusts them forward, perfectly poised to drive its talons deep into the flesh of its prey. For many small animals, the impact of this sudden piercing of their vital organs is lethal, and those that survive the first blow are usually too stunned to put up much resistance. The victim, which the hawk may consume on the spot or carry off, is sometimes an amphibian or a snake. More often hawks prefer small mammals, and mice are a favorite. The relatively small American kestrel, for example, eats nearly three hundred mice in the course of a year.

Only a few species, like the Cooper's hawk (below), are bird killers, but they have given all their fellows a reputation among farmers as "chicken hawks." As a result these raptors have long been a favorite target of rural hunters. In attempting to protect their coop, however, many farmers have misguidedly shot their top mouser.

To ward off other predators, many hawks cover, or mantle, their kill with their wings. At left, a female Cooper's hawk mantles a bobwhite quail she has just downed.

Eagles: View from the Top

From their lofty perches atop tall trees or mountain crags at heights seldom visited by most other species, two birds are the undisputed masters of all they survey in North America—the only eagles native to the continent. One of these great birds lives only in the New World—the bald eagle (left), national emblem of the United States. The tawny-headed golden eagle (opposite) has a larger range, which also includes the northern regions of the Old World.

Before the arrival of Europeans in North America the domains of this princely pair, which are approximately the same size, extended from Hudson Bay to Panama. But the rise of cities and especially the spread of farms killed off much of their natural prey and, along with extensive hunting, forced them to retreat into the few remaining pockets of wilderness. Today the bald eagle is populous only in Alaska, although a few nest in other parts of the country, especially California and Florida. The golden eagle is also numerous in Alaska, but farther south it has largely withdrawn to the slopes of the Rockies.

Perched on the branch of a tree that has already lost most of its foliage to Alaska's October chill, a bald eagle (left) enjoys an unobstructed view of the evergreen forest below. Opposite, a golden eagle surveys the meandering canyon of the Snake River from a rocky palisade.

Lords Aloft

Few creatures have so inspired men as the giant golden eagle, with its awesome seven-foot wingspan, one of the largest and strongest birds of prey in the northern hemisphere. As a symbol of nobility and valor, its image topped not only the standards of the legions of Imperial Rome but also the totem poles of the Indians of the Pacific Northwest, where it was known as Thunderbird. This powerfully built raptor, called golden because of its russet-colored hackles, preys mainly on small to medium-sized mammals, especially the jackrabbits and ground squirrels that abound in the open plains and valleys adjacent to the mountains where it builds its eyrie. But the golden eagle will sometimes attack animals much larger than itself, even full-grown deer and antelopes, if they are weak or snowbound.

Glistening in the sun as it soars over a shadowy Idaho mountainside, a golden eagle (opposite) searches for prey in a territory that it will not share with any other member of its own species except its mate. In this exclusive domain the eagles build cliffside eyries, like the one at right, which they inhabit and renovate over a period of years and which may grow to measure more than five feet across and to weigh more than a ton.

THE TURKEY VS. THE BALD EAGLE AS A NATIONAL BIRD: TWO VIEWS

by Benjamin Franklin

As a patriotic symbol, the epitome of nobility, strength and valor, the eagle has represented more nations than any other creature. It was only natural, then, that the founding fathers of the United States should select the American bald eagle as the appropriate representation of their fledgling republic. But one of their number, the venerable Benjamin Franklin, registered a strong demurrer. In a letter to his daughter, reprinted below, Franklin set forth his reasons for feeling that the eagle was unworthy of being the national bird. Audubon, the great artist-ornithologist, saw the bald eagle in a more sympathetic light. Audubon's case for the big bird is excerpted here from Ornithological Biographies.

For my part, I wish the bald eagle had not been chosen as the representative of our country; he is a bird of bad moral character; he does not get his living honestly; you may have seen him perched on some dead tree, where, too lazy to fish for himself, he watches the labor of the fishing-hawk; and, when that diligent bird has at length taken a fish, and is bearing it to his nest for the support of his mate and young ones, the bald eagle pursues him and takes it from him. With all this injustice he is never in good case; but, like those among men who live by sharping and robbing, he is generally poor, and often very lousy. Besides, he is a rank coward; the little king-bird, not bigger than a sparrow, attacks him boldly and drives him out of the district. He is therefore by no means a proper emblem for the brave and honest Cincinnati of America, who have driven all the *kingbirds* from our country; though exactly fit for that order of knights which the French call *Chevaliers d'Industrie.*

I am, on this account, not displeased that the figure [appearing on the Order of Cincinnatus medal] is not known as a bald eagle, but looks more like a turkey. For in truth, the turkey is in comparison a much more respectable bird, and withal a true original native of America. Eagles have been found in all countries, but the turkey was peculiar to ours; the first of the species seen in Europe being brought to France by the Jesuits from Canada, and served up at the wedding table of Charles the Ninth. He is, besides, (though a little vain and silly, it is true, but not the worse emblem for that,) a bird of courage, and would not hesitate to attack a grenadier of the British Guards, who should presume to invade his farmyard with a *red* coat on.

by John James Audubon

The great strength, daring, and cool courage of this Eagle, plus his unequalled power of flight, render him highly conspicuous among his brethren. Had he a generous disposition towards others he might be looked up to as a model of nobility. His ferocious, overbearing, and tyrannical temper is, nevertheless, best suited to his state, and was wisely given him by the Creator to enable him to perform his offices.

Imagine yourself floating gently down the Mississippi at the approach of winter, amid millions of water fowl approaching on whistling wings from the north to seek a milder climate. The Eagle perches erectly on top of the tallest tree beside the broad stream, while with glistening, stern eye he surveys the vast expanse. He listens attentively to every sound, now and then glancing down to earth, lest the light tread of the fawn pass unheard. His mate is perched on the opposite bank, and, should all be tranquil and silent, she warns him by a cry to continue patient. At this he partly opens his broad wings, inclines a bit downwards, and answers in tones not unlike the laugh of a maniac. Then he resumes his erect attitude and silence returns.

Ducks—the Teal, the Wigeon, the Mallard and others—pass in great rapidity, following the course of the current. The Eagle heeds them not. They are then beneath his notice. But the next moment, when the wild, trumpet-like sound a yet distant but approaching Swan is heard, the female Eagle comes shrieking across the stream. The male suddenly shakes all of his body before beginning to arrange his plumage with a few touches of his bill. The snow-white bird is now in sight, her long neck stretched forward, her eye watchful as that of her enemy. With seeming difficulty her large wings support her weight, flapping incessantly. So irksome do her exertions appear that her very legs are spread beneath her tail to aid her flight. But she approaches, and the Eagle marks her for his prey. As she passes the dreaded pair, the male starts from his perch with an awful scream that brings more terror to the ear of the Swan than the report of a large duck-gun.

Witness the Eagle's powers as he glides like a falling star and comes upon his timorous quarry like a flash of lightning. The Swan, in agony and despair, seeks by various manoeuvers to elude the grasp of his cruel talons, mounts, doubles—would willingly plunge into the stream were she not prevented. The Eagle, long possessed of the knowledge of such a possible stratagem for escape, attempts to strike her from beneath with his talons, to keep her in the air. The Swan, much weakened and with strength failing at the sight of the courage and swiftness of her antagonist, soon gives up hope. She gasps as the ferocious Eagle strikes the underside of one of her wings with his talons and forces her to fall in a slanting direction on the shore. See the cruel spirit of this dreaded enemy of the feathered race. He exults over his prey, presses his powerful feet downward, and, all the while shrieking, drives his sharp claws deeper than ever into the heart of the dying Swan. The female Eagle watches her mate's every movement. If she did not assist him in the capture, it was not from want of will but merely from the assurance that the power and courage of her lord were quite sufficient for the deed. She sails to the spot, and together they feast.

Although they stand out here against grassy backgrounds, the crowned eagle (above) and the harpy eagle (right) are camouflaged in their normal rain-forest habitat, with dappled plumage that blends well with thick foliage. In fact, the harpy's disguise is so effective that it is rarely seen in the wild. The distinctive crest feathers of the crowned eagle, however, make it a more visible target and a highly prized catch for African hunters, who use the feathers for personal adornment.

Unlikely-looking Raptors

Although the two round-faced birds on the facing page resemble owls and the sad-looking bird above has such a unique appearance that it would seem to occupy its own private niche in the animal kingdom, all three are eagles. The fact is not immediately obvious because the ample feathers of their crests and napes hide their bullet-shaped eagle heads. The nearly extinct monkey-eating eagle (above) lives in the Philippines, while the slightly more numerous crowned eagle (opposite, left) dwells in central and southern Africa and the harpy eagle (opposite, right) makes its home in equatorial South America.

Though they live in such widely separated parts of the world, these unlikely-looking eagles have a lot in common. All three inhabit tropical rain forests, where their principal prey are monkeys and other small mammals. And they are all well adapted to life in their habitat's dense foliage. Short, broad wings and long, squared-off tails enable them to rise almost vertically between the trees and to maneuver with speed and agility through the branches and vines. Unlike other eagles, they seldom soar, but they do nest in the highest spot available—usually in the tops of the giant trees that project above the canopy of the forest.

47

This prairie falcon—legs thrust forward for landing (above) and pulled
back during takeoff (opposite)—shares the plains and mountains of the
American West with eagles, hawks and other falcons.

Falcons: The Sky Raiders

With their slender, streamlined bodies and long, pointed wings, falcons are superbly suited for aerial combat and, among all the birds of prey, are the uncontested masters of the midair kill. Preying mostly on other birds over unwooded terrain, a falcon, cruising or perched, waits patiently until its quarry reaches just the right altitude—sometimes after being driven out of the relative safety of the bush by the falcon's mate and hunting partner. Then the falcon streaks from the sky and delivers a deadly blow to the neck with its talons, hitting with such force that its victim is sent hurtling to the ground.

Such high-velocity power-diving "stoops" would be fatal to the falcons themselves if they were striking prey on or near the ground. The peregrine falcon, which ranks among the world's fastest animals, has been clocked stooping at speeds of up to 175 miles an hour.

High-rise Squatters

Sheltering a clutch of young gyrfalcons whose juvenile feathers are just beginning to poke through their snowy infant down, the mountain ledge above is typical of the sites that falcons choose for nesting. It has a protective overhang and is high enough to be well out of the reach of most predators. Since falcons never build their own nests, the gyrfalcon nestlings are squatting in a secondhand eyrie that their mother probably occupied early in the spring before the original builders—very likely a pair of ravens —could reclaim it. Some falcons do not even bother to take over other birds' nests, laying their eggs instead on bare rock ledges. The female peregrine at right made do with a flower-filled crevice in a sheer cliff for her clutch, which contains two hatchlings and one still unhatched egg.

Condors: Soaring Scavengers

With gnarled, leathery hide covering its head, the Andean condor of South America (opposite) certainly does not rank among the most beautiful birds, but it does hold a record for size. A 10-foot wingspan and a weight between 20 and 25 pounds make it the largest of the flying land birds. And, like its slightly smaller cousin farther north, the California condor (right)—now dangerously close to extinction—the Andean condor is one of the most accomplished soarers in the realm of birds, surpassing even the golden eagle with the majesty and ease of its flight.

Both of these enormous mountain-dwelling birds fly only during the heat of the day when the rising currents of warm air give them the lift they need to buoy their great bulk. Then these members of the New World vulture family sail over the surrounding foothills, valleys and plateaus at an easy 30 miles an hour searching for the carcasses of cattle, sheep, deer and llamas, which they will eat no matter how putrid. But condors, like most vultures, are quite clean. The California condor bathes frequently in mountain streams and is often seen perching with its wings outspread to absorb the disinfecting rays of the sun.

An Andean condor (opposite) displays two of the features that adapt this vulture to a life of carrion-eating: a head free of plumage that could collect filth and a small, arched bill for efficiently snipping away at meat and tendons. The deeply slotted wing tips of the California condor (right) help it soar gracefully by counteracting air turbulence.

Clean-up Squad

Vultures are nature's garbage collectors. In the tropical and subtropical regions where they abound, vultures provide a swift and efficient form of natural sanitation by disposing of the dead and decaying remains of animals. In the jungles of South America, the reigning scavenger is the king vulture (opposite), the possessor of one of the most bizarre and colorful of avian faces. Although this bird is only two thirds the size of its close relative, the great condor, it earns its name by being the largest vulture in its domain.

Since larger vultures such as the king get first pick at mealtime, smaller species have adapted to the occasional scarcity of their normal food. Some species have even learned to make do on palm nuts when carrion is unavailable. One of the most extraordinary adaptations, however, is demonstrated by the Egyptian vulture, shown in the four pictures on this page. This remarkable bird has discovered how to use a stone to crack ostrich eggs, establishing it as one of the few animals other than man to use tools.

A young Egyptian vulture demonstrates the remarkable tool-using ability of this species in the three pictures at left. After repeatedly picking up a large pebble with its bill and hurling it at an ostrich egg, the bird finally succeeds in cracking the tough 1/16-inch-thick shell. But an adult (above) pushes in to get the first helping of egg.

Owls

Armed with the keenest vision in the animal kingdom, birds usually rely on their eyesight more than any other sense. Most fly forth at daybreak and become quiescent when visibility wanes at nightfall. But not all birds are day creatures. Two major orders of land birds, the Strigiformes (owls) and the Caprimulgiformes (nightjars, oilbirds, potoos and frogmouths), plus a handful of isolated individuals, such as the kiwi and kakapo of New Zealand, have become nocturnal.

The most compelling reason for their adaptation to the night shift is the abundance of food available under cover of darkness, when a host of small, warmblooded animals goes abroad and insects abound. It may have been in pursuit of such prey that the ancestral owls and nightjars first ventured into the night.

With one notable exception, all are predatory feeders—owls hunting much the same small game as hawks and eagles, the nightjars feasting on insects. The lone exception, the guacharo, or oilbird, subsists on ripe fruit, which is just as available by day as by night; yet the oilbird is wholly nocturnal and the most accomplished of all night fliers. Burrowing deep in limestone caves of Trinidad and South America, oilbirds were discovered by the German naturalist Baron Alexander von Humboldt and named for their incredibly fat young, which once supplied the Indians with oil for lamps and cooking. Within the somber labyrinths of their underground warrens oilbirds get around through a system of echolocation like that used by bats, making a rapid clicking sound that is audible to human ears. They are the only birds able to navigate well in absolute darkness.

Possibly more than any other order of bird, the 146 species of owls are most easily recognized by their family resemblance. All have the hooked beak and sharp talons of diurnal birds of prey and use them in the same way, but it is the large head, absence of neck and, most of all, the wide, solemn, forward-staring eyes that emphatically say "owl."

Owl eyes are even bigger than they seem to be. The yellow iris and black center are the only visible parts of the very large eyeballs, which almost touch inside the center of the bird's extraordinarily wide skull. Owls' eyes are so sensitive that they can discern objects in light 10 times dimmer than the lowest visual threshold of human sight. The notion that an owl's blinking eyes are blind by day is a myth. Their daylight capability is usually more than adequate, for though owls hunt at night, they almost never hunt in total darkness. The moon, stars, aurora borealis, the dimmest glow of sunset and predawn are sufficient to enable an owl to get about easily.

But what about overcast nights in thick pine forests where some owls hunt? Even there some dim light exists, but to help eyes strained to the limit of perception, owls have a backup location system, a highly developed sense of hearing. Ear openings on the sides of their wide heads—not be to confused with the tufts or "horns" that adorn some owls—work somewhat like human ears. A sound coming from one side or the other reaches the nearest ear a split second before the other ear. But where humans merely interpret such a delay to form a general idea of direction, owls can fix the source of a sound and locate prey with absolute precision. In many owls the ear openings are slightly asymmetrical, an arrangement that may help the birds to judge distance as well as direction.

There are other, less obvious aids to night hunting. Soft, sound-muffling flight feathers and a large wing area in relation to weight enable owls to fly in almost complete silence. The advantage is twofold: They can surprise prey and are better able themselves to pick up sounds. When they are not hunting, though, owls are anything but silent. Their repertory of blood-curdling screams, hoots, whistles, coughs and screeches has linked the birds through the ages with witches and hobgoblins. Their night sounds are sometimes territorial warnings to other males or, more often, mating calls.

An equally familiar night sound is the courtship plaint of the whippoorwill, a member of the nightjar family. Seeking to attract a mate, the bird repeats its name over and over at roughly one-second intervals. Some nightjars, birds of wide distribution in tropical and temperate regions, gather insects the way whales feed on plankton, cruising the night sky with gaping, bristle-flanged mouths. Goatsucker is another name for the breed (it was once supposed that the birds used their capacious mouths to steal milk from goats). During the day, most nightjars settle on the ground, where their mottled brown feathers render them virtually invisible. Tropical members of the clan, the potoo of South and Central America and the frogmouths of Australia and Southeast Asia, achieve the same invisibility by perching on the broken ends of branches, where they become to all appearances extensions of the limbs.

Great horned owl

The Diversity of Owls

Although they seem to look very much alike, there is considerable variety in the size and coloration of the world's 146 species of owls, cosmopolitan birds that inhabit every continent except Antarctica. The largest species belong to the family of eagle owls, which includes the nearly two-foot-long great horned owl of North America (above) and the equally large Malaysian eagle owl (opposite, left).

Among the smallest of the owls is the seven-inch saw-whet (opposite, right) from North America. The plumage of the majority of owls is perfectly adapted to the birds' nocturnal life-style. Shades of gray, black, brown and white predominate in patterns that range from patches and stripes to bands or streaks. Such coloration is an effective camouflage for these forest and mountain dwellers.

Great horned owls (left) and their close relative, the Malaysian eagle owl (below), have tufts of feathers on their heads that are not a part of their actual organs of hearing, which are not visible. These beautifully dappled birds are primarily night-hunters, flying along the edges of forest clearings in search of such prey as grouse, ducks, skunks and rodents.

The delicate saw-whet owl (above) is one of the many species of owls that embark on occasional migrations, sometimes covering considerable distances. In winter these birds roost in the refuge of evergreen trees. From a lookout point on the limb of a tree the saw-whet spots its prey, mostly mice, as well as small birds and insects.

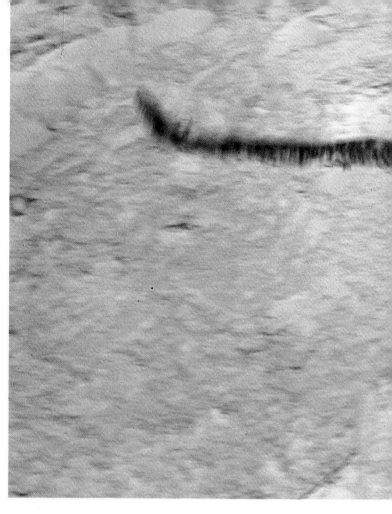

With eyes at half mast, a Javan brown wood owl shows off its impressive head turn. Owls are the only birds that blink the way humans do—by lowering their upper lids. When they go to sleep, however, like all birds, they close their eyes by raising their lower lids.

Night Hunter

Owls are among the most successful nocturnal predators by virtue of a number of extraordinary anatomical specializations. Dominating the owl's flattened facial disks are the splendid eyes that are its basic hunting equipment—large, forward-facing orbs that give the owl the widest field of binocular, or three-dimensional, vision among predatory birds. Since owls cannot rotate their eyes, they must turn their heads in order to see to the side or rear and can swivel more than 180 degrees in either direction (left).

Silent flight (above) is another owl adaptation, useful in taking prey by surprise and made possible by soft body feathers and tiny filaments that cover the edges of the flight feathers and act as mufflers. Not all owls are quiet fliers, however. The birds that hunt by day, such as the burrowing owls (right), cannot rely on stealth and invariably have feathers that rustle audibly when they take to the air.

Owls swallow their prey whole and then cough up the indigestible fur and bones of their victims in the form of pellets (below). Pellets, usually found directly beneath their roosts, are a good way to determine the whereabouts of owls. In the case of burrowing owls (bottom), diurnal desert- and prairie-dwellers from North, Central and South America, pellets often mark the entrance to the underground holes these birds inhabit. The birds either take over the abandoned burrows of mammals or lizards or dig their own to use as brood chambers for their young.

The Faithful Ones

Once they have mated, a pair of owls often remain together for life, returning year after year to the same nesting site to lay their eggs. All owls produce round, white eggs, but the size of the clutch varies from one to 12, depending on the species and the availability of food. The female, which is considerably larger than her mate, lays her eggs over a period of several days and begins incubating the first one as soon as it is laid. The eggs hatch one at a time, in the order in which they were laid. The process results in the older chicks having an advantage over their smaller, weaker siblings in the competition for food.

When they hatch, chicks are blind and helpless, and are covered with white down. They develop a downy transitional plumage before the adult coloration appears. The black-feathered faces of the short-eared owl chicks below, for example, will eventually turn tawny like those of their elders, and by the age of 12 weeks they will resemble their parents.

Heart-shaped facial disks distinguish barn owls from all other owls. The disks and the first flight feathers begin to show through the chicks' down when they are about six weeks old (right). About six weeks later, barn owls can learn to fly. For another four weeks they are dependent on their parents to supply food, which is a demanding job—the growing chicks can consume their own weight in food each day.

Tawny owls incubate their eggs and raise their chicks (left) in nests either in tree hollows, rock crevices, attic walls or in the abandoned burrows of foxes and badgers. The tawny owl is widespread in Europe. A nonmigratory bird, it inhabits both woodlands and rocky terrain.

A Varied Bag of Visual Tricks

The goatsuckers, or nightjars, are short-legged and long-winged. Insect-eating birds with huge gaping mouths, they tend to hunt at dawn and dusk and sleep during the day. Like many nocturnal birds, they have a somber, dappled plumage of browns and beiges—coloration that helps conceal them from predators.

Included in the Caprimulgiformes order are the potoo (left), an inhabitant of the West Indies, Mexico, Central and South America; the common nighthawk (opposite, below) of North America; and the poor-will (opposite, above) of western North America, one of the few birds known to hibernate. As autumn gives way to winter and the insect population dwindles, the poor-will creeps into crevices and hollows in canyon walls. Its temperature drops gradually from 102° to about 65° F., its heartbeat becomes indiscernible and its usually high metabolic rate almost ceases. With the return of warm weather the poor-will wakens from its torpor.

Neck outstretched, eyes half closed, a potoo (left) blends perfectly with the tree stump on which it sits. Unless approached too closely, the bird will remain motionless in this position until it perceives that danger has passed. Broken tree stumps are also used by the potoo to cradle its single spotted egg. Both members of a breeding pair share the duties of incubation as well as taking part in the rearing of their down-covered chick.

A common nighthawk (opposite, bottom) lays a parental wing over its chick and flattens its body on its nest, depending on plumage that resembles the forest floor to fool the eyes of any passing predator. This adaptable bird has reacted to a shrinking habitat by successfully substituting the flat rooftops of office buildings for its natural woodland nesting spots. It is now a familiar sight in many cities and towns.

Hummingbirds

Like aircraft that engineers have strengthened with spidery trusses and sheathed in aluminum, birds that fly have evolved all sorts of ways to cut their body weight and increase their flying ability. The extraordinary strength-to-weight ratio of a feather is obvious to anyone who handles one. Less apparent but equally effective weight-savers are birds' hollow bones, internal air-filled cavities, the substitution of beaks for teeth, the laying of eggs (which relieves the female birds of the burden of carrying a developing embryo) and even the shrinkage of the sex glands between breeding seasons.

Some birds bear an increased load as the result of special aerial adaptations and must find still other ways to jettison weight. Two prime examples are swifts and hummingbirds, the pursuit plane and helicopter of the avian world. Each has a propulsion system so powerful and relatively heavy that it has in part forfeited its landing gear. Swifts are classified as Apodiformes—footless ones—but both swifts and hummingbirds have tiny, nearly useless feet. The bones, tendons and minute claws are there, but the muscles that control them have become so small in the interest of flight that the birds are virtually unable to walk.

Swifts, as their name implies, are very fleet of wing. Plummeting falcons can match or surpass the 150 miles per hour reported for the largest swifts—the thrush-sized, spine-tailed species of eastern Asia—as they dart about in pursuit of insects, but no other small birds can come close to such speeds in sustained flight. There are 86 known species of swifts, found nearly everywhere on the globe. All are keen insectivores, with flattish streamlined heads and long swept-back wings that often extend well beyond the tail when the birds are at rest.

They rarely are. Swifts are believed to spend more time airborne than any other birds. One, the common swift, has been observed flying all night long without once coming to rest. When they do alight, swifts land on vertical surfaces, which they cling to the way a picture hangs on a wall. Their sharp toenails serve as hooks and their stiff, stubby tails as props below. Cliffs, rock crevices, hollow trees and, since the entrance of modern man into their world, the insides of chimneys (from which the chimney swift takes its name) are favorite roosts.

Nesting on a vertical surface presents special problems. A few species utilize small ledges, but most solve their dilemma with glue. The mucilage they use is their own saliva. Snatching up twigs and leaves on the fly, they make a kind of reinforced cement, which they mold into a bracketlike nest. Certain swiftlets of Malaya and Indochina make their nests entirely of saliva, and it is from these edible nests that Chinese cooks make bird's-nest soup.

Hummingbirds have evolved a form of flight unique in the avian world. Other birds can hover for a moment or two if they have to, but the darting, start-stop, up-down, forward-backward flight of hummers belongs to them alone (page 12). Utilizing this faculty, hummers scull the air rather than stroke it, gaining constant lift from what is more of a forward-and-backward movement than the more usual up-and-down flapping of other birds. When hovering, hummers' bodies assume a nearly vertical position. Dipping their long beaks into a nectar-filled blossom, they seem to be almost standing in midair.

To power such an extraordinary set of wings, which never have a rest when the bird is in flight, hummers have the largest pectoral, or chest, muscles for their size of any animal alive. They represent a full 25 to 30 percent of the birds' total weight. The price the hummers pay—along with the swifts—is diminished musculature in the legs. Hummingbirds do perch, but they almost never move along a branch or spring into the air in the way that most perching birds do.

Though male and female swifts are look-alikes, most male hummingbirds outshine the females to a spectacular degree and are thoroughly polygamous. Perhaps because they are so small and, with few exceptions, have developed no alluring love song, hummingbirds have evolved into the jewels of the avian world. "Glittering fragments of the rainbow," Audubon called them, recognizing that their iridescence depends on the refraction of the sun's rays. Once a male hummer has impressed a female with a spectacular show of dives and swoops, carefully staged to catch the sun on his resplendent bib or burnished head, he quickly mates and leaves her for another. And as befits such polygamous behavior, the males are fiercely territorial. Secure in their aerial ability, they fear no other birds and will attack intruding parrots, hawks and crows as readily as their own rivals.

Hummingbird on Bonaire Island in the Caribbean

The Sundancers

Homing in on a hibiscus blossom, a black-chinned hummingbird hovers motionless on wings that appear like blobs of mist to the naked eye, while its long tongue probes for nectar. Most hummingbirds seek out "hummingbird flowers"—usually blossoms that are as vividly colored as the birds themselves, with bell-shaped petals that will not hinder their whirring wings.

On a cloudy or rainy day, hummingbirds are inconspicuous birds indeed, with drab, dark plumage that fades into the shadows. But given a ray of sunshine, their gorgeous feathers spring to life in glinting, iridescent colors that have no match in nature. In 19th-century Europe hummingbird feathers were in such demand as ornaments for women's hats and jewelry that their tiny pelts were imported by the millions from South America, and for a time some species of the little birds were threatened with extinction. Fortunately, the vogue ended, and most of the hummers survived.

Superb aerialists, hummingbirds court, mate, eat, drink and fight on the wing. The only times they stop their dancing flight are when they rest and when they are nesting (overleaf). Whether coming in easily for a perfect two-point landing (above) or veering smartly to the right in search of a new blossom, Anna's hummingbird, named for a 19th-century French duchess, is the equal of any flier in the family.

Expandable Nest

All of the 338 species of hummingbirds build dainty nests of lichens, mosses or leaves, lined with thistledown or soft plant fibers, which are lashed to a limb with cobwebs and molded to the shape of the mother bird's breast. Exactly two white eggs, the size of jelly beans, are deposited in each nest, and the mother broods for two weeks or longer, until the naked, blind chicks are hatched. The female parent does all the work. After fertilizing her eggs, the male has nothing further to do with family life.

As the tiny nestlings grow and sprout their pinfeathers, they fill their demitasse-sized nest snugly, like the two black-chin chicks above, but the nest is flexible enough to expand with them. The growing young need a constant diet of protein-rich insects, and the mother, like the blue-chested hummingbird at left, is hard pressed to keep up with their appetites, as well as satisfy her own hunger.

A nesting ruby-throated hummingbird lacks the crimson collar that distinguishes her mate. Ruby-throats, the only hummingbirds native to the eastern United States, nest as far north as Quebec and may fly 2,000 miles south, across the Gulf of Mexico, to winter—a prodigious feat.

Parrots and Parakeets

Not all parrots are tropical, but all tropical forests are rich in parrots. Flamboyant arboreal birds, raucous of voice and gaudy of color, most parrots seem to embody the very essence of hot exotic lands. Even the names are evocative: parrot, parakeet, cockatoo, cockateel, lory, lorikeet, macaw, lovebird, budgerigar.

There are 336 living species of parrots. The smallest are the pygmy parrots of Papua, no bigger than wrens. The largest are the Amazonian macaws, some as tall, head to tail, as a five-year-old child but not big enough to save them from becoming the occasional meal of the powerful harpy eagle. Among all these diverse birds, certain traits are common. These include large heads, short necks, sharply hooked beaks and powerful, prehensile feet. When parrots fly they move very fast, as if to get it over with quickly. Most are not fond of foraging on the ground but climb nimbly around in trees, using their beaks as a third claw. Parrots are gregarious and usually travel through the forest in flocks. They chatter to each other as they go, using sound to identify their own kind.

In an age before the jet plane shrank the world and television introduced nature's wonders into the living room, a scarlet macaw from the Amazon jungles brought a special feeling of delight, exoticism and vicarious adventure to a coal-heated parlor in Manchester, England, or Boston, Massachusetts. The bird balanced on the prehensile toes of one foot while with the other it held food up—first to a cocked eye and then, if it approved of the morsel, to that outrageous beak. And on top of all that, the marvelous apparition would, on command and as often unbidden, croak out the recognizable syllables "Polly want a cracker."

Long before Marco Polo and Christopher Columbus brought them to Europe, parrots were domesticated by primitive tribes of Africa and Asia. Although some species have succulent flesh—Norfolk Island parrots met the fate of man-made extinction because they were good to eat—it was less for their value as food or for any other service they might render than for their companionship that the gaudy birds won a place in man's family circle. Other animals were domesticated initially for some form of servitude—to provide food or clothing, to carry burdens or transport men's vehicles and machines, to hunt game, destroy insect pests or catch rats. But parrots appear to have captured the fancy of humans through sheer personality and good looks. And the feeling is mutual: Parrots actually seem to enjoy being in the company of people.

Yet, however gorgeous the chained macaw or engaging a billing pair of caged lovebirds may appear beside a potted palm, they pale by comparison to a flight of wild military macaws hurtling pell-mell and in full voice through the Central American forest or a sulphur-crested cockatoo filling the New Guinea jungle with screeches from the branch of a banyan tree.

In captivity, parrots' imitative urge induces them to copy human speech—or the sound of a vacuum cleaner or telephone bell. Sounds once learned are likely to be repeated for life. And if it happens to be the sound of the telephone, that can mean a lot of rings, for parrots are extremely long-lived in captivity—50 years is not extraordinary and 80 has been reported in one case.

Today, parrots and their kind range around the equatorial belt, though they once penetrated as far north as North Dakota in the New World and to France in the Old. Their northern limit today is Mexico and Central Asia.

The order Psittaciformes ("Psitta" is Greek for "parrot") is mostly vegetarian, but insects, grubs and worms supplement the diet. The kea, a dull-colored parrot of the New Zealand highlands and sometimes a scavenger, recently acquired a dangerous taste for sheep. At first it was content with sheep carrion, but later it learned to prey on the live animals, landing on their backs and pecking into their kidney fat. As a result, the government put a bounty on the bird, and it is now extremely rare.

Another New Zealand parrot that belies all the generalities is the kakapo, which feeds mostly on the ground under the cover of darkness. The kakapo climbs trees to get at fruit and berries and uses its wings to glide back to the ground again, but beyond that it has completely lost the power of flight. It too appears to be on the way to extinction as man encroaches on its forest habitat.

The Carolina parakeet, a native North American species, has already become extinct. The last of them was seen in the Florida Everglades in 1920. Some 12 inches long, with a yellowish-green body and an orange-yellow head, it was a handsome and relatively common member of the bird population of the United States. But it ate grain and fruit crops and incurred the wrath of farmers, and it also tempted sportsmen who valued it as a game bird. As a hunter's target, it had the unfortunate habit of hovering in sympathetic flocks over a fallen bird, allowing a hunter to mow down an entire flock with a few loads of buckshot.

*Top, left—sulfur-crested cockatoo; top, right—military macaw;
bottom, left—red and green macaw; bottom, right—blue and yellow macaw.*

Gaudy Giants

Largest of all the parrots, because of their long, serrated tails (left), are the 15 species of macaws. Brightly colored creatures that are found throughout Central and South America, macaws of many species can be distinguished by the large, bare patches of skin that ring their eyes. In macaws, unlike some other parrots, the sexes usually display no difference in appearance; the male and female (below) are look-alikes.

Primarily forest-dwellers, macaws have been hunted since the time of the Incas, who treasured their brilliant feathers as adornments. Their large curved beaks are powerful enough to crack even the rock-hard Brazil nut and also serve as a "third foot" in climbing through the branches of trees. The powers of imitation that have made parrots so popular are greatly limited in the macaws, who rarely learn more than a few words.

Trooping of the Colors

The name "parrot" conjures up visions of splashy color against a jungle background, and it is true that the majority of the family live up to their reputation as tropical birds in fancy dress, though some are downright drab in appearance and at least one, the kea of New Zealand, lives in mountain highlands. Some are marked by vivid splotches of color, like the thick-billed parrots of Mexico, at left, with their scarlet foreheads, cheeks and shoulders. Others, such as the hawk-headed parrot (opposite, right), are splendidly plumed with several hues that subtly merge from maroon to brown to blue and green. The two parrots profiled opposite, left, are an unusual example of parrot color dynamics. The green bird below is a male eclectus parrot, and the more flamboyant redhead above is his mate. They were long believed to be separate species. With their bright visors and epaulets, the thick-billed parrots at left have a military appearance that befits their flight patterns in tight V-formation echelons. Denizens of the pine forests of Mexico's Sierra Madre mountains, they formerly flew in flocks of several hundred as far north as Arizona. They have fallen victim to the heavy deforestation of their habitat and live on, in greatly reduced numbers, as threatened species in only a few mountain fastnesses.

Gregarious birds, the thick-billed parrots flock together each morning in screeching flights of as many as 1,000 birds, and again at night when they roost together in the tall pines of their mountain home. Their fondness for pine nuts frequently results in plumage that is sticky and matted with resin, not at all like the sleekly groomed pair at left.

A striking scarlet, blue-splotched parrot of the New Guinea and Australian rain forests (above) and another lettuce-green bird (below) were described as separate breeds until hunters realized that the green parrots were all males and the red invariably females. Only then did ornithologists reclassify the two as the same noisy eclectus parrot.

When an interloper intrudes on its territory, the male hawk-headed or red-fan parrot of northern South America and the Amazon River basin (right) raises its head and neck feathers in a fearsome threat display. In repose, the hawk-head's ruff settles smoothly against its head, and it looks like an ordinary parrot.

Comfortable with Man

The smaller members of the parrot family, including parakeets, lorikeets and lovebirds, have generally adapted well to the presence of man and his works and many are popular, amiable cage birds. At least one of the small fry—the budgerigar of Australia—is possibly more numerous today in cages and aviaries of Europe and North America than it is in the wild. The seven-inch red-backed parrot of southeastern Australia (right) is a gregarious bird that flocks in great numbers to nest in fields and gardens. Because it eats few grains and fruits, the red-back is not regarded as a pest and has established a comfortable relationship with humans.

The Caribbean parakeets (left) inhabit the arid ABC islands of the Dutch Antilles, and, although they all belong to the same species, they have a curious local head coloration that varies according to their particular island of origin. On Aruba their heads are olive green, on Bonaire they are orange-capped and on Curaçao the identifying color is yellow.

The Caribbean parakeets shown at left feasting on the fruit of a cactus habitually nest in the towers built by termites, with no apparent objection from the original tenants. The red-backed parrot, seemingly covering its blushing backside with its wings at right, may also select a termite hill for a nesting site, but it is just as likely to pick a tree cavity or a man-made birdhouse. During the mating season red-backs go through a common ritual: The male selects a likely spot and then brings his mate to inspect it, but only when she approves will the pair start to build their nest.

Rose-ringed parakeets, distinguished by the delicate pink circlets around their necks, gather together on a tree in India. Gregarious little birds, they flock together in great numbers and often settle in gardens and tilled fields on the fringes of civilization. They are the most widely distributed of all parrots, inhabiting lands of the Old World from West Africa to Indochina. Rose-rings were the first parrots to reach Europe, brought to Greece by a helmsman of Alexander the Great's fleet.

81

My Senegalese Birds and Siamese Cats

by James Thurber

Lovebirds, as everyone knows, are expected to present a picture of twittering bliss in a cage. Not so with the pair of birds acquired by James Thurber and his wife. They not only failed to live up to the lovebird stereotype, they frankly "hated each other's guts." How the dilemma of the loveless lovebirds was resolved is recounted here in a mood of quiet desperation, the humorist's hallmark.

I have been going through some yellowing recollections and old dusty whereabouts of mine, with the vague idea of setting down my memoirs now that I am past sixty, and it comes to me with no special surprise that none of them is stained with blood or bright with danger, in the active, or Hemingway, sense of the word. My experiences, like those of most sedentary men fond of creature comforts such as steam heat and room service, have been distinguished by an average unremarkableness, touched with grotesquerie, discomfort and humiliation, but definitely lacking in genuine .50-caliber peril. I have never "met the tiger face to face," as Kipling once put it, or climbed anything higher and colder than half a dozen flights of stairs, or struggled all afternoon to land a fish that outweighed me by three hundred pounds. It occurs to me, however, that some of the most memorable adventures of any man's life are those that have had to be endured in a mood of quiet desperation. I am reminded, for specific example, of a quietly desperate night I spent more than twenty-five years ago on the Blue Train running from Paris to Nice.

After my wife and I had become comfortably ensconced in our sleeping quarters on the train (you can't become ensconced any other way, come to think of it) we discovered, to our dismay, that our Couchette, or Sleepette, or whatever it was called, was to be shared by a short, middle-aged Frenchman, who scowled all the time, occasionally muttered to himself, and didn't even look at us.

My wife had bought, in a Paris flower market, God knows why, two Senegalese love-birds which hated each other's guts, and she had insisted on bringing them along. Before we all retired, practically at the same moment—and don't ask me how we managed it—our unexpected companion had kept glancing nervously at the bird cage, which my wife had suspended from something. We had had the two birds for about three weeks and the male had never burst into song, although we had been told that he would. We had gradually come to the conclusion that he couldn't stand his mate, had had no say in her selection, and did not intend to serenade her, or even admit that she was there. They would sit side by side all day long on their little wooden swing, not swinging or ruffling a feather, or even looking at each other, just staring into some happier past. In our hotel room in Paris they had slept all night long, motionless and indifferent to each other, and to us. On the train to Nice they decided, out of some atavistic impulse, to fan out their wings all night long, with intervals of only a few seconds between their rufflings. In such cramped lodgings, about eight by five, the noise they made was the noise of half a dozen Pullman porters busy with whisk brooms. I can still hear clearly their continual *flut, flut, flut.* It began to get me, it began to get my wife, and it began to get the Frenchman.

Our roommate had gone to bed, composed himself on his back, and pulled on a pair of black cotton gloves. He had then closed his eyes and gone quietly to sleep in a facile way that we envied. He wasn't to sleep long, however, for the flutting began about fifteen minutes after the light had been turned out. The male would flut, and then the female would flut, and then they would flut together. For birds who had never flutted a single flut in three weeks, they turned out to be surprisingly good at it, deeply interested in it, and utterly tireless. After about twenty minutes of the flutting, the Frenchman snarled, "It is necessary to cover those birds." My wife, who spoke excellent French, told him that the birds had been covered, and he suggested that she put something else over their cage. This, she explained to him after groping for the word, would cause them to suffocate. The Frenchman said something in a threatening tone that I didn't get, but which was later translated by my wife as, "It is as well to suffocate as to be strangled." I got up and put my coat over the cage, but the flutting came through as clearly as ever. All night long the three of us would doze off, wake up, and doze off again. Each time the Frenchman woke up he had a different expression, and he ran through everything from *"zut alors"* to what might be roughly translated as, "If a merciful Providence does not silence those birds, I shall throw them off the train and myself after them." (My wife assured me in a whisper that he had said "myself" and not "you.")

Two weeks after we got to our hotel in Nice, we were awakened at dawn one morning by the sound of a bird singing. The sound came, astonishingly enough, from our bird cage, and the song was loud, gay, and full-throated. We got out of bed to explore this incredible phenomenon and discovered that the female was lying dead on the floor of the cage. Whether she had died of boredom, or heartbreak, or had been slain by her hitherto mute "mate," we never, of course, found out. A few days later, we decided to give the male away, cage and all, to an old woman who was selling birds in the flower market of the old town. She was suspicious at first of two Americans who had only one lovebird and who wanted to get rid of it for nothing. "Does he sing?" she asked us doubtfully. My wife didn't have an answer ready for that, but I did. "He sings," I told her, "at funerals." This was literally true. I had decided to bury the dead bird in the garden of the hotel, but I had not known how to get it out to the garden without arousing the suspicion of the French proprietress, a suspicion than which there is none stronger or more durable in the world. Finally, in a kind of elaborate panic,

which is customary with me, I had put the unfortunate creature in my pocket and had taken along the cage with the other bird in it. "What in the name of God for?" my wife had asked me, reasonably. "To divert suspicion," I told her. "I will say I am taking him out for an airing. You come too." To this she replied firmly, "No." I managed to bury the dead bird—it was night and the garden was deserted—without attracting onlookers, although I recall that the proprietress seemed relieved later on when we finally checked out of the hotel. The bird in the cage had sung at the funeral not a dirge but an unmistakable roundelay or madrigal, probably a Senegalese version of "She is gone, let her go, God bless her."

The old woman at the flower market stared at me coldly when I mentioned funerals. Experience had doubtless taught her that the line is thinly drawn between American comedy and American insanity. My wife turned away to examine some flowers, with the air of a woman who has become disillusioned and is planning to vanish. I made the mistake, as I always do, of elaborating, and my elaboration in French is something to hear. I think I used the phrase *"goutte de tristesse,"* which literally means "drop of sorrow" and had, as you can see, only the faintest bearing on the situation. Thinking I might be arrested if she allowed me to proceed in my reckless French, my wife rejoined us and came out with the true story of the short unhappy life of the diminutive parrots, ending with a brief account of the mysterious death of one of them. The old woman's eyes lighted with understanding, and she pointed out that the other bird had probably been a male too. This, she added, took the case out of the realm of *crime passionel* and into the realm of *sang-froid.* Since the case was plainly not going to be taken to court, the theory, however sound, seemed immaterial and academic. My wife suddenly broke the silence by demanding twenty-five francs for the survivor. This put the old woman on familiar ground. We began to haggle and compromise. She agreed, in the end, to take the bird for nothing, but her tone was aggrieved. She wanted us to know that she had come off badly, for, as she pointed out, where in the world would she get a Senegalese lovebird as a companion for this solitary male?

The Cockatoos

The forests of Australia and Malaya are full of cockatoos, the only parrots with fanlike crests of feathers on top of their heads. Most of the 16 species are white, though some have feathers washed with tints of pink or yellow. In some species, such as the sulphur-crested cockatoo seen here, the color of the crest contrasts vividly with the bird's stark-white plumage.

The sulphur-crested cockatoo is typical of most of these parrots. A fairly large bird measuring 18 inches in length, it makes its nest in a tree cavity, where both male and female share the duties of incubating the clutch of two to four eggs.

Whether perched serenely on the limb of a tree (above) or flying gracefully above the forest canopy (right) the sulphur-crested cockatoo is a common sight to the natives of New Guinea. Noisy, gregarious birds, they are often found in large flocks.

Pigeons and Doves

The gentle dove, symbol of peace, has endured a most violent struggle to survive. Four notable species of the order Columbiformes—the passenger pigeon, the dodo, the Rodriguez solitaire and the Réunion solitaire—have been exterminated by predators with a taste for squab, man among them, and nine others are either endangered or presumed extinct.

And yet, despite all the harassment they have experienced—the killing of mourning doves is estimated at 49 million per year—and their seemingly weak defenses, birds of the family Columbidae, the pigeons and doves, have generally managed to survive and even proliferate in every part of the world short of the polar regions. A few species, such as the rock dove, have been widely propagated by man and liberated outside of their native lands. Rock doves are now among the commonest of city birds despite efforts to exterminate them or drive them away and have taken over parks and public plazas and buildings from St. Mark's in Venice to the Capitol dome in Washington. Rock doves have been domesticated for their young squabs or (in an earlier time) for their usefulness as airborne messengers. In 1815 the news of Napoleon's defeat at Waterloo was first brought to England by homing pigeons, five days before the first surface messengers arrived.

The distinction between doves and pigeons is largely a matter of local nomenclature. But generally birds with larger well-rounded bodies are referred to as pigeons, while the name "dove" is reserved for the smaller, more streamlined birds. In size the 303 surviving species range from the diamond dove of Australia, only eight inches long, hardly bigger than a house sparrow, to the magnificent crowned pigeon of New Guinea, large as a hen turkey. This pigeon has dwindled because of its habit of perching in trees and simply ignoring hunters.

Two distinguishing features of pigeons are the way they drink and a unique manner of feeding their young. Most birds scoop up a beakful of water, raise their heads and let it run down their throats. By contrast, pigeons suck up water without lifting their heads. To nourish their young, which are born naked and helpless, the parents produce pigeon's milk, a white, curdlike substance. Though it provides much the same nutritive value as mammal's milk, it is actually a sloughing off of the lining of the bird's crop. This special adaptation frees the pigeon parents from some of the burden other birds must bear, constantly hunting for high-protein food for their nestlings. Another distinct advantage is a high and constant fertility rate that gives pigeons a biological advantage over physically tougher species such as parrots. Pigeons are monogamous, and most indulge in a comical "bow and coo" courtship rite when they breed, which may be as frequently as four times a year but usually occurs no more than twice. Male pigeons help their mates in nest-building and the upbringing of the young. If brooding pigeons are interrupted in raising a brood—as often happens, since man is not alone in savoring squab meat—they start a new family without delay.

At one point the most prolific breeder among pigeons—and perhaps all birds—was the American passenger pigeon, which resembled a mourning dove, although it was half again as large. Before the white man began to shoot, net and smoke them out of trees with sulphurous torches, there may have been more passenger pigeons in North America than all other birds put together. Their numbers, according to some estimates, ran into the billions. They nested in the deciduous forests of the Northeast in mass colonies that sometimes measured 20 miles across. Their migrations darkened the sky. They broke limbs from large trees by the sheer weight of numbers. Yet, when subjected to the white man's hunting practices and encroachment on their habitat, the passenger pigeons vanished entirely. The last one died in the Cincinnati Zoo in 1914.

Almost as notorious was the tragic extinction of the largest of the pigeon family, an ungainly, flightless bird of the remote Indian Ocean island of Mauritius. Sixteenth-century Dutch sailors who stopped there to provision their ships called the creature *dod-aarse*, or dodo. For hundreds of thousands of years the big, awkward birds, descended from an ancestor of the pigeon, had had free run of the island without a single predator to menace them. Dodos weighed up to 50 pounds, waddled about on stocky feet and were weird looking enough to figure in *Alice in Wonderland*. They were easy to kill with clubs, stones and guns. A single dodo would feed 25 hungry seamen. But in the end—which came in the 1680s, just 174 years after Mauritius was discovered—it was not man's direct hand alone that finished the breed but the pigs and monkeys he brought to the island. These attacked the dodo where a bird is most vulnerable—in the nest. Unlike most pigeons, the trusting dodo nested on the ground, where it laid a single bun-sized egg, an easy mark for the alien predators.

Snow pigeons

The Far-flung Fraternity of Pigeons

The cosmopolitan character of pigeons and doves is illustrated by the sampling on these pages. The lavender-hooded green-winged pigeon is an eastern Oriental, with a range that extends from China to Australia. The shy bleeding-heart pigeon, with the distinctive "wound" on its breast, is a native of the Philippines, and the pink-breasted Picazuro inhabits woods and open country from northeastern Brazil to the suburbs of Buenos Aires. Halfway around the world again, the spectacled Comoro blue pigeon is one of a group of related fruit doves that make their home on remote islands of the Indian Ocean. The turtledove of Biblical and poetic renown has long been a familiar bird of the Mediterranean littoral and southern Europe. And the closely related spotted sandgrouse, which has the head of a pigeon and the body of a partridge, but is not a true pigeon, is a native of South Africa.

Peripatetic though they may be, the birds have had varying degrees of good and bad fortune when they have crossed the path of man. Sandgrouse, once widely distributed over much of the eastern hemisphere, have been heavily hunted and have nearly disappeared from southern Europe, where they were once abundant. The bleeding-heart, on the other hand, is easily domesticated and is a favorite cage bird in the Orient. The green-wing, which shares part of the bleeding-heart's range, has never adapted well to the presence of man and meets a peculiar death in considerable numbers by dashing into whitewashed walls and wire fences. Comoro blue pigeons are still fairly common in the forests of the Comoro Islands but are so widely hunted that ornithologists fear they may soon meet the fate of their nearly identical cousin, the Mauritius blue pigeon, which is now extinct. Both turtledoves and Picazuro pigeons have held their own with civilization and live close to man. But as the dodo or passenger pigeon bear mute witness, coexistence with mankind can be a chancy matter for some of the less adaptable birds of peace.

Spotted sandgrouse

Turtledove

Green-winged pigeon

Bleeding-heart pigeon

Comoro blue pigeon

Picazuro pigeon

Two doves that live in close association with man are that familiar of the barnyard, the Old World rock dove (left) and the North American mourning dove (opposite), which live in an "edge" habitat, close to civilization. Rock doves are the progenitors of 200 kinds of domestic pigeons, including the pouters and fantails, which have been bred for racing, food and show for thousands of years. Mourning doves, unlike their close cousins, the extinct passenger pigeons (pages 92–97), have managed to survive and even thrive in farmland even though they are prime targets for game-hunting sportsmen.

The Passenger Pigeon

by John James Audubon

Over a century ago passenger pigeons dominated American bird-life. Their nesting sites became the haunts of hunters and the scenes of wholesale slaughter. In 1813 Audubon witnessed such a scene in Kentucky and described it in Ornithological Biographies. *A century later, in 1914, the passenger pigeon was extinct.*

The multitudes of Wild Pigeons in our American woods are astonishing. Indeed, after having viewed them so often and under so many circumstances, I now feel inclined even to pause and reassure myself that what I am going to relate

is fact. Yet I have seen it all, and in the company, too, of persons who like myself were struck with amazement.

In the autumn of 1813 I left my house at Henderson on the banks of the Ohio, on my way to Louisville ninety miles distant. In passing over the Kentucky barrens a few miles beyond Hardinsburg, I observed the Passenger Pigeons flying from northeast to southwest in greater numbers than I had ever seen them before, it seemed to me. Feeling an inclination to count the flocks that might pass within the reach of my eye in one hour, I dismounted, seated myself on an eminence, and began to mark a dot with my pencil for every flock that passed. In a short time, finding this task impracticable because the birds were pouring by in countless multitudes, I arose. But before I travelled on, I counted the dots that I had put down and found that one hundred and sixty flocks had been recorded in twenty-one minutes. I met still more, farther on. The

air was literally filled with Pigeons, and the noon-day light was obscured as by an eclipse. The dung fell in spots not unlike melting flakes of snow; and the continuous buzz of wings tended to lull my senses.

While waiting for dinner at Young's Inn at the confluence of Salt River with the Ohio, I saw, at my leisure, immense legions still going by. Their front reached far beyond the Ohio on the west, and the beechwood forests directly east of me. Not a single bird alighted, for not a nut or acorn was that year to be seen in the neighborhood. Consequently they were flying so high that different attempts to reach them with a capital rifle proved ineffectual; nor did the reports disturb them in the least. I cannot describe to you the extreme beauty of their aerial evolutions when a Hawk chanced to press upon the rear of a flock. At once, like a torrent, and with a noise like thunder, they rushed in a compact mass, pressing upon each other towards the center. In these almost solid masses they darted forward in undulating and angular lines, descended to the earth and swept close over it with inconceivable velocity. Then they mounted perpendicularly so as to resemble a vast column, and, when high, they were seen wheeling and twisting within their continued lines, which resembled the coils of a gigantic serpent.

Before sunset I reached Louisville, fifty-five miles from Hardinsburg. The Pigeons were still passing in undiminished number. They continued to do so for three days in succession. The people were all in arms, and the banks of the Ohio were crowded with men and boys incessantly shooting at the pilgrims, which flew lower as they passed the river. Multitudes were thus destroyed. For a week or more, the population fed on no other flesh than that of Pigeons, and talked of nothing but Pigeons.

It is extremely interesting to see flock after flock per-

forming exactly the same evolutions which a preceding flock has traced in the air. Thus should a Hawk charge on a group at a certain point, the angles, curves and undulations described by the birds in their efforts to escape the dreaded talons of the plunderer are undeviatingly followed by the next flock that comes up. Should the bystander happen to witness one of these a frays and be struck with the rapidity and elegance of the motions, and desire to see them repeated, his wishes will be gratified if he but remain in the same place until the next flock of Pigeons comes along.

As soon as the Pigeons discover a sufficiency of food to entice them to alight, they fly around in circles, reviewing the countryside below. During these evolutions the dense mass which they form presents a beautiful spectacle, as it changes its direction, turning from a glistening sheet of azure, as the backs of the birds come simultaneously into view, to a suddenly presented, rich deep purple. After that they pass lower, over the woods, and for a moment are lost among the foliage. Again they emerge and glide aloft. They may now alight, but the next moment take to wing as if suddenly alarmed, the flapping of their wings producing a noise like the roar of distant thunder, as they sweep through the forests to see if danger is near. However, hunger soon brings them to the ground. On alighting they industriously throw aside the withered leaves in quest of the fallen mast. The rear ranks continually rise, passing over the main body and alighting in front, and in such rapid succession that the whole flock seems still on the wing. The quantity of ground swept in this way is astonishing. So completely has it been cleared that the gleaner who might follow in the rear of the flock would find his labor completely lost. While feeding, their avidity is at times so great that, in attempting to swallow a large acorn or nut, they may be seen to gasp for a long while as if in the agonies of suffocation.

When the woods are filled with these Pigeons, they are killed in immense numbers, although no apparent diminution comes of it. About mid-day, after their repast is finished, they settle on the trees to enjoy rest and digest their food. On the ground and on the branches they walk with ease, frequently jerking their beautiful tails and moving their necks backward and forward in the most graceful manner. As the sun begins to sink beneath the horizon, they depart *en masse* for the roosting place which, not infrequently, is hundreds of miles away, a fact ascertained by persons who have kept track of their arrivals and departures.

Let us inspect their place of nightly rendezvous. One of these curious roosting places on the banks of the Green River in Kentucky I repeatedly visited. As always, it was in a part of the forest where the trees were huge and where there was little underbrush. I rode through it for more than forty miles, and on crossing it in different parts I found it rather more than three miles wide on average. My first view of it was at nearly two hours before sunset, about two weeks before the coming of the Pigeons. Few of these birds were then to be seen, but a great gathering of persons with horses and wagons, guns and ammunition had pitched camp on the edge of the forest.

Two farmers from the vicinity of Russellville, more than a hundred miles distant, had driven more than three hundred hogs to be fattened on the Pigeons they hoped to slaughter. Here and there, people were busy plucking and salting birds already killed, and they sat amid large piles of them. The dung lay several inches deep, covering the whole roosting place. I noticed that many trees two feet in diameter were broken off at no great distance from the ground; and the branches of many of the largest and tallest had given way. It was as if the forest had been swept by a tornado, proving to me that the number of birds must be immense beyond conception.

As the time of the arrival of the Passenger Pigeons approached, their foes anxiously prepared to receive them. Some persons were ready with iron pots containing sulphur, others with torches of pine knots; many had poles, and the rest, guns. The sun went down, yet not a Pigeon had arrived. However, everything was ready, and all eyes were fixed on the clear sky which could be glimpsed amid the tall tree-tops.

Suddenly a general cry burst forth, "Here they come!" The noise they made, even though still distant, reminded

me of a hard gale at sea, passing through the rigging of a close-reefed vessel. As the birds arrived and passed over me, I felt a current of air that surprised me. Thousands of the Pigeons were soon knocked down by the pole-men, while more continued to pour in. The fires were lighted, then a magnificent, wonderful, and almost terrifying sight presented itself. The Pigeons, arriving by the thousands, alighted everywhere, one above another, until solid masses were formed on the branches all around. Here and there the perches gave way with a crash under the weight, and fell to the ground, destroying hundreds of birds beneath, and forcing down the dense groups of them with which every stick was loaded. The scene was one of uproar and confusion. I found it quite useless to speak, or even to shout, to those persons nearest to me. Even the gun reports were seldom heard, and I was made aware of the firing only by seeing the shooters reloading.

No one dared venture nearer the devastation. Meanwhile, the hogs had been penned up. The picking up of the dead and wounded birds was put off till morning. The Pigeons were constantly coming, and it was past midnight before I noticed any decrease in the number of those arriving. The uproar continued the whole night. I was anxious to know how far away the sound could be heard, so I sent off a man used to roaming the forest, who returned in two hours with the information that he had heard it distinctly three miles from the roosting place.

Towards the approach of day, the noise somewhat subsided. Long before I could distinguish them plainly, the Pigeons began to move off in a direction quite different from the one in which they flew when they arrived the evening before. By sunrise all that were able to fly had disappeared. The howling of the wolves now reached our ears, and the foxes, lynxes, cougars, bears, raccoons, opossums and polecats were sneaking off. Eagles and Hawks, accompanied by a crowd of Vultures, took their place and enjoyed their share of the spoils.

Then the authors of all this devastation began to move among the dead, the dying, and the mangled, picking up the Pigeons and piling them in heaps. When each man had as many as he could possibly dispose of, the hogs were let loose to feed on the remainder.

97

Cavity Dwellers

Birds are most vulnerable in the nest—a grim truism of avian life borne out by the fate of the dodo and a host of other extinct species. To protect this weakest link in their life cycles, camouflage and inaccessibility in their nesting places are the birds' basic strategies. The so-called cavity-nesters, such as hornbills, bee-eaters, woodpeckers and toucans, build their nests and lay their eggs in hollow trees or in ground burrows.

The smaller cavity-nesters select or cut holes just big enough to squeeze into, thereby excluding all larger predators. The larger birds have bigger problems. None solves them better than the hornbills, although they seem to pay a terrible price in discomfort for the female and exhaustion for the male. Hornbills inhabit the tropical regions of the Old World. They can grow large (up to five feet long) and are ungainly looking creatures, with outsized downcurved bills which in mature birds are sometimes surmounted by horny growths. In nesting, most hornbills first find a hollow in a large tree, then employ a unique device for protecting the eggs: walling up the female inside the hole. Before the female lays eggs, she and the male work together on the wall, using a mixture of mud, excrement and bits of vegetable matter. As the job progresses, the female must remain inside, where she lays her eggs. Finally, the opening is sealed, save for a tiny peephole just large enough for the tip of the male hornbill's beak to pass fruit and insects to his mate through a barrier that has the impregnable consistency of brick.

When the young hatch, usually two to four per nest, the male must increase his pace; he is a bedraggled and exhausted bird by the time his mate emerges to help him finish rearing the nestlings. Having taken half a day to chip her way free, the mother hornbill emerges stiff but well dressed in a new suit of feathers; her annual molt coincides with her confinement. Then the young, unaided, seal themselves up again for another few weeks.

Hornbills belong to the order Coraciiformes. Another delightful member of the order is the bee-eater. More than half of the 44 species live in Africa; the rest are scattered across the warmer regions of the Old World. They are pretty birds, about the size of a thrush, decked out in pastel greens, blues, russets and golds. Their beaks are long, pointed tweezers used to snap up insects of all kinds, particularly bees.

Bee-eaters nest in holes in the ground, usually excavated into the sides of vertical banks, often in large colonies. In digging the burrows and even feeding the young, some species of bee-eaters are cooperative, and sometimes two or more younger unmated male birds help a nesting pair.

Bee-eaters are often the victims of another group of birds that shares much of their range and their interest in bees: the honey-guides. They lay eggs in the bee-eaters' nesting hole, in the manner of Old World cuckoos and New World cowbirds. Newly hatched honey-guides have sharp hooks on the tips of their beaks with which they dispatch their competitive bee-eater nest companions; then the hooks drop off. Some honey-guides have an extraordinary appetite for beeswax. Unable to break into hives themselves, they form a symbiotic partnership with honey-loving animals like the ratel, or African honey badger. A bird leads the way to the hive, chirruping and flitting about, and then waits patiently while the ratel destroys the hive and eats the honey, leaving the wax for the birds.

Honey-guides are classified with woodpeckers in the order Piciformes. Like owls, woodpeckers have keen ears that enable them to locate bark beetles and boring insects by the sound they make chewing wood. Woodpeckers' chisel bills and stiff tails, which they use to position themselves as they hammer at trees, are familiar sights. But the most unusual adaptation of the 204 species of woodpeckers is rarely seen: their long tongues, which they insert anteater-fashion into the insect chambers to winkle out the succulent grubs. Some woodpeckers, known as sapsuckers, feed by drilling holes in trees to release a flow of sweet sap. They return again and again to a tree they have tapped days before and feed not only on the sap but also on the insects attracted by the sap.

Another Piciforme, and a cavity-nester from the New World tropics, is the toucan, well known for its clownish manners and enormous bill—an admirable instrument for picking fruit and a natural model for cartoons of nosy birds. The machete-shaped bill may be preposterously oversized —in one species, the toco of the Brazilian rain forest, almost half the size of the bird consists of its bill—and plays a part in the courting and social rites of toucans. When they are playing, a troupe of toucans will often break off into pairs and have at one another, parrying and thrusting with their bills with all the spirit and enthusiasm of expert fencers but never actually with an intent to kill and always apparently in the spirit of fun and sport.

Red-headed woodpecker

Drummers of the Forest

Woodpeckers are the wood nymphs of the bird world. They make their homes, raise their young and find most of their food in the trunks of trees. More than any other birds, they have successfully invaded tree trunks and have flourished in the forested lands of every part of the world except Australia, the Oceanic islands and Madagascar. Their dependence on trees has become so great, in fact, that some woodpeckers are disappearing in proportion as their woods vanish. The large, handsome ivory-bill approaches extinction with the progressive deforestation—over the last half century—of the large stands of timber it once inhabited in Cuba and southeastern United States.

Other members of the woodpecker family, however, such as the great spotted woodpecker of Europe and the familiar red-headed woodpecker of eastern North America, have continued to thrive, hammering out a rolling tattoo that is as much a part of the woodland scene as the trees themselves. Indians of the American West likened the woodpecker's drumming to thunder and believed that the perky birds were rainmakers—and indeed the rat-a-tat of the Gila and yellow-fronted woodpeckers does sound something like distant thunderclaps. Actually, the drumming serves the same purpose as some of the vocalizations made by other birds—as a warning to invaders of a bird's territory or as an alluring mating call.

The nine-inch great spotted woodpecker is one of a "sympatric pair," amiably sharing its particular tree with the six-inch lesser spotted woodpecker. A female Gila woodpecker, a bird of southwestern desert lands, brings a meal of berries to her eager nestlings. The red-headed woodpecker is nearly omnivorous, eating fruit and flying insects as well as the grubs of tree-boring insects. The gaudy yellow-fronted woodpecker, a close relative of the red-headed, inhabits woodlands from northeastern Argentina to southern Brazil.

Gila woodpecker

Red-headed woodpecker

Yellow-fronted woodpecker

The Birds and the Bees

Small, brightly colored birds that make their homes in subdeserts, swamps and savannas, the bee-eaters are extremely sociable and flock together in groups that usually number 50 to 60 birds, although colonies of as many as 25,000 have been observed.

All bee-eaters dig underground warrens, such as the pueblolike structure above, in a bank along the Niger River of central Africa, which is the home of a colony of carmine bee-eaters. The burrows invariably end deep underground in large oval egg chambers, and the parents may be assisted in the care and feeding of the young by other members of the community with no offspring of their own to look after. The nestlings are fed a bland diet of harmless insects at first and are gradually weaned to the honeybees and other stinging insects, the staple foods of adults that have given bee-eaters their name.

Side by side, a pair of cinnamon-chested bee-eaters (right) scans the horizon for passing insects, which they catch on the wing and then carry to a perch for a leisurely meal. The bee-eaters' voracious appetite for honeybees is shared by another family of birds, the remarkably similar jacamars of South America. Together, bee-eaters and jacamars.share a unique ecological niche.

As fastidiously as a diamond cutter handles a tiny gem, a carmine bee-eater (left) holds a honeybee in its tweezerlike bill. Before consuming the dangerous tidbit many bee-eaters render it harmless by gingerly rubbing the bee against their perch until the sting breaks off. Carmines are able to neutralize bees-stings as they fly, but how they perform such a midair operation is an ornithological mystery.

103

Bill Collection

The toucans of South and Central America are among the most improbable-looking of birds. Not even their close cousins the hornbills (overleaf) or the pelicans can match them when it comes to profiles. Those massive bills have long been a puzzle to ornithologists. They may serve as a means of identification to birds of the same species, and they may play some role in courtship, although the prenuptial rites of toucans appear to be no more than an exchange of fruit between prospective mates. As defensive weapons the great bills are clumsy and inefficient, although their appearance may be quite effective in scaring off some predators.

One scientific conjecture has it that toucans' bills originally evolved to consume some long-extinct giant fruits or insects and are still used for picking the fruit the birds subsist on. The most flamboyant of the family is the keel-bill, or rainbow-billed toucan (above), with a profile that may include every color of the rainbow except violet.

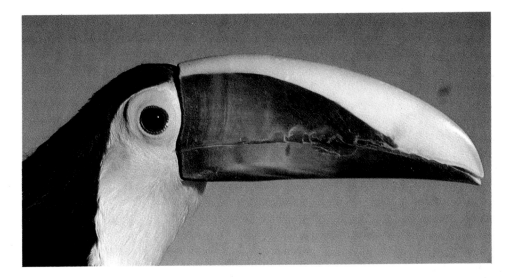

Swainson's toucan (left), like all the larger crow-sized birds of its tribe, has a bill that is intricately constructed of bony fiber like the wicker basket of a jai-alai player, combining surprisingly light weight with strength. Swainson's toucan, also called the chestnut-mandibled toucan, ranges from Honduras to northern South America.

The toco (right) and the keel-bill (opposite) have the largest bills of all toucans—nearly equal to their body length. When they prepare to sleep, toucans literally fold up, turning their heads 180 degrees, stretching their bills along their backbones and covering them with their long tails.

Cuvier's toucan (left), another of the family's largest-billed members of the genus Ramphastos, builds its nest in the hollows of trees in tropical jungles. Though nesters may remove rotten wood to improve their nests, Cuvier's toucans do little if any chiseling with their bills in the manner of their woodpecker cousins.

Bare-faced Birds

The Old World hornbills, like their American counterparts the toucans, are natural comedians. The oversized bills of many species are surmounted with a bony protuberance, or casque, set like a helmet in the big birds' foreheads. Some have faces which are naked and often vividly colored, and they are among the few birds with eyelashes. The white-crowned hornbill of Indonesia (opposite, top) sprouts a feathery cockade in lieu of a casque, and others, like the young wreathed hornbill of equatorial Asia, below, make do with unadorned bills. All but two of the 45 species of hornbills keep their families sealed in walled-up tree cavities during the annual breeding season.

The casques serve no apparent purpose. Most are made of porous horny material, but the helmeted hornbill of Borneo has a casque of solid ivory, which natives carve into fetishes. Because hornbills are easily tamed, African villagers often make pets of them, and because they apparently mate for life and are devoted parents, the big birds are regarded as sacred models of virtue and are never molested by the villagers.

The young white-crowned hornbill above has just begun to grow the feathered tiara that distinguishes mature birds. More typical of the family is the great hornbill of southern Asia (right), with its helmetlike topping and a giant land snail in its beak. Hornbills are omnivorous, many of them foraging the forest floor for insects, fruits, lizards and small mammals. During the nesting season, a harassed male will fill his craw with as many as 50 figs at once and make up to 70 trips daily to feed his imprisoned family.

Cuckoos

The two-note mating call of the common cuckoo has given the order Cuculiformes a name for eccentric behavior and made "cuckoo" a synonym for mental disorder. But cuckoos are anything but crazy; they have an instinct for survival that has helped them to adapt and thrive in almost all temperate and tropical parts of the world, from rain forests to deserts. Certain cuckoos have given the family a bad, and somewhat unfair, reputation by laying their eggs in the nests of other birds, but not all cuckoos are brood parasites; the great majority, in fact, build their own nests and rear their young in the fashion of most other birds.

The Cuculiformes are a large and varied order that includes 149 species and such disparate types as the roadrunner of the American Southwest, the emerald-green touraco of the African jungle and the European prototype for the Swiss cuckoo clock, the common cuckoo. They bear such arresting names as the bare-faced go-away bird, which does indeed scream "go away!" and warns the creatures of the African bush country of approaching predators or human hunters. Many a game expedition has been frustrated by the go-aways.

Most cuckoos are arboreal insect-eaters, and some are long-distance fliers of remarkable stamina, but the American roadrunner and its close cousin, the ground cuckoo, stick closely to the earth as much as possible and take to the air only when absolutely necessary. The roadrunner, with its incredible running speed, can outmaneuver any dog or fox, running with head stretched forward and tapering tail pointed aft, cackling at its pursuers in a voice that sounds like an insane laugh. It feeds on snakes, small mammals and large insects that it hunts through the dry desert scrub. A few ground cuckoos parasitize the nests of other birds, but not the roadrunner.

Those cuckoos that are brood parasites do their dirty work with consummate skill and apparent calculation. The Anglo-Saxons, an earthy tribe well in tune with the creatures of fen and forest, recognized the cuckoo's seeming duplicity with the word "cuckold." In the spring the female cuckoo, having responded to the hiccoughing call of her mate, sets out on a detailed survey of her territory, carefully observing her potential hosts, whose nests may number from 20 to 30. She watches them build their nests, sometimes flying right down for an inspection when the other birds are away.

Just as the mating ritual of other birds stimulates ovulation, the female cuckoo's close observations trigger her own egg-laying. She must deposit her egg within a day of the time the prospective foster mother lays her own clutch in order for the young cuckoo to hatch in time to be competitive. She waits until the unsuspecting nesters are away, usually in the early afternoon, and then swoops down and quickly lays a single egg. At the same time she often takes away one of the eggs in the host's clutch, either eating it on the spot or dropping it as she flies away. She repeats the process at approximate 48-hour intervals until she has deposited eggs in as many as a dozen different nests.

When the parents return, if all goes well for the cuckoo, they notice nothing untoward and will incubate and raise the changeling as their own. The cuckoos tend to choose hosts whose eggs resemble their own, and the hosts differ in different regions. According to J. C. Welty's *The Life of Birds*, "In Finland the cuckoo lays bright blue eggs, and its chief hosts are the redstart and whinchat . . . both of which lay blue eggs. In Hungary, the cuckoo lays greenish eggs boldly blotched with brown and black, and so does its chief dupe, the great reed warbler. . . ."

When the cuckoo hatches it resembles most other nestling birds, blind and able to gape for food, but that is as far as the resemblance goes. When it is about 10 hours old, an uncanny instinct asserts itself by means of a shallow depression on the little cuckoo's back. If any solid object, such as an egg, a young bird or even an acorn, touches this sensitive spot, the blind baby bird thereupon pushes it out of the nest. The interloper continues the process until it has cleared the nest. It is then alone to take all the food its foster parents can bring.

In the case of the shining bronze cuckoo of the South Pacific, the fledging of the young bird marks the start of a feat of navigation that defies the imagination. The shining bronze cuckoos parasitize the nests of tiny nonmigratory flycatchers on the outlying islands of New Zealand. Adults lay their eggs and immediately fly north, toward the equator. A month later they are joined by the young they have never seen. To accomplish their remarkable rendezvous the fledgling cuckoos may fly 1,200 miles over the sea to Australia and then another 1,000 miles to the Solomon and Bismarck islands. They do this themselves, with no parent birds, real or foster, to show them the way. How they accomplish their incredible journey is one of the great ornithological mysteries.

Hartlub's touraco

Enfants Terribles

The female cuckoo's search for an unwitting "host" to incubate her eggs, once thought to hinge entirely on her finding eggs that are similarly colored to her own, is now believed to be a function of a process called imprinting. The female seeks out a surrogate mother of the same type that raised her. Other complexities of the cuckoo's peculiar brood-parasitic behavior remain a mystery. It is known, for example, that individual cuckoo females produce eggs that are always the same color, but it is not fully understood how different females of the same species may lay eggs that are dissimilar. Other puzzles are how many eggs a cuckoo lays and how she distributes them, but one study suggests the cuckoo's potential: Over a two month period, a single cuckoo female laid 25 eggs in the 25 different nests of a meadow pipit.

A hedge sparrow (above), dwarfed by its baby cuckoo, stands on the cuckoo's back to feed it. At right, a reed warbler tries a different approach. In spite of the size differential—quarter-ounce birds sometimes raise cuckoos until they weigh almost a quarter pound—the cuckoo's yawning maw triggers irrespressible feeding instincts in the foster parent.

110

A mature dunnock arrives with food for a hungry cuckoo chick (left). After 21 to 23 days, the hatchling leaves the nest but will continue for another three weeks to beg for food—from its foster parents or any other bird unable to resist its gaping pink mouth.

A cuckoo hatchling, blind and naked, instinctively overpowers its dunnock nest mates and struggles to push one over the side. Because it will multiply its weight some 40 to 50 times before it leaves the nest, it needs all the nourishment smaller adults would normally provide for several of their own chicks.

A roadrunner scans the landscape in the Mojave Desert, California. State bird of New Mexico, the roadrunner is inquisitive and cunning, whether poking around the tents of campers or lying in wait near water to pounce on a swift in midair when it descends to drink.

112

Legendary Westerners

Roadrunners, desert-dwellers of the American Southwest, do not, as folklore has it, build a trap of cactus spines around a snake and wait for it to impale itself. Nor, if snake-bitten, do they ingest a special herb as an antidote. They do kill snakes—even rattlers—as well as almost any other small creatures. Stalking birds, rodents, lizards and scorpions is made easier by the roadrunners' powerful legs, which can carry them at speeds of 15 to 20 miles an hour.

Roadrunners are not brood parasites. They build their own nests—large, untidy affairs of cow dung, snakeskins and vegetation—during the breeding season. The period is signaled by the appearance of red, white and blue skin behind the birds' eyes, as seen in the photograph at right and in the drawing above by Roger Tory Peterson.

Cranes

"To every thing there is a season, and a time to every purpose, under the Heaven," says the Old Testament's Book of Ecclesiastes. In the Biblical sense, cranes are birds whose time and season may have passed. Stately, long-legged, deliberate and unruffled, they appear strangely out of place in a world that throbs to man's tempo. The sight of cranes flying, long necks and feet extended, cruising in chevron formation half a mile high over Russia's Valley of the Volga or across the dry arroyos of the American Southwest, harks back to more primitive times.

During the Pleistocene epoch, a half million years ago, the cranes, or Gruidae, were a much larger order of birds. Today there are only 15 species left, and five of those are in severe danger of extinction. The whooping crane is one of the rarest birds in North America, numbering fewer than 100 birds. The only other New World crane, the sandhill, ranges as far north as Alaska and the Siberian coast and as far south as Cuba; the common crane and the pretty little demoiselle winter in Africa and live in Europe during the warmer months. One species, the brolga, inhabits Australia and New Guinea; all the rest are natives of Asia and Africa, where a very few appear to have made accommodation with man, while others live in shrinking habitats on borrowed time.

Hunting is partly responsible for the decline. But the plow and the drainage ditch have been far more destructive than sportsmen. Most cranes are migratory birds, and the routes they follow between their winter and summer grounds each year become more hazardous and less hospitable with the advancement of civilization. Disruption of the breeding grounds and migratory routes can effectively spell the end of a particular breeding stock. Depending on their ability to change or detour, they bow to an inflexible law of nature: adapt or die.

The two North American cranes dramatically exemplify the principle. In winter, the smaller, dove-gray sandhill has learned to find sustenance in man's cut-over corn and wheat fields. As a result, with the added protection of game laws, migrating sandhills appear to be holding their own. The more aquatic whooping crane, gleaming white with black wingtips and red head, is less flexible in its ways. The backbone of its range once stretched across the central plains, from Canada to Louisiana, now prime farm land. Though omnivorous, the whooper feeds mainly on aquatic animals. Marsh and swampland are its natural home, and as they disappeared, so did the cranes. By 1941 there were only 15 wild birds left, living in winter on the Aransas National Wildlife Refuge on the Gulf coast of Texas and breeding no one knew where.

A strenuous effort on the part of conservationists and the discovery in 1954 of the whooper's breeding site in Wood Buffalo National Park in Alberta meant that both termini of the big bird's lifeline could be protected from human predation. Experiments are now underway to establish a second group of whoopers by a process called cross-fostering, in which whooper eggs are placed in sandhill nests to be hatched and raised like the baby swan in the story of the ugly duckling. It is hoped in this way to start a second colony of whoopers within the sandhill flocks in case some natural disaster wipes out the remaining wild population, which now numbers roughly 55 birds.

All species of cranes are stilt-legged with flexible, serpentine necks and strong pointed beaks. With their sharp weapons they probe into the waters of bayous and uplands for tender shoots, roots, grubs, worms and crustaceans, supplemented occasionally by small fish and rodents. In defending their nest, usually a raised mound in the middle of a marsh, whooping cranes will fight to the death. They have been known to kill predators as large as wolves by spearing them through the eye.

The dance of the cranes is among the most graceful and riveting sights in all of nature. Among mature prospective partners, male and female address each other as in a formal cotillion with elaborate bows; then, alternately arching their long necks and throwing their heads backward, they leap into the air. These *jetés* propel the birds eight to 15 feet into the air, and their feathery bodies float down in slow motion. They land on the tips of their three forward-pointing toes. Dancing reaches a frenzy at the peak of the mating season, when the *pas de deux* may continue for many minutes at a time. The first round of dancing is apparently a rite to cement a partnership that will last for life, and after that, with birds already paired, dancing appears to awaken the dormant mating urge.

Curiously for an endangered, skittish order, most cranes adapt well in captivity, becoming quite tame and breeding readily. Exotic African and Asian species such as the crowned crane of the Nile Valley and the huge sarus are common sights in many Western zoos. And it may be that zoos and even the protected reservations where the whooping cranes winter offer the only future the magnificent birds may have.

Crowned crane

Crown of Gold

The eastern crowned crane is a well-known wetlands inhabitant of eastern and central Africa. With its downy black forehead, pink cheeks and extraordinary stiff golden crown of feathers, it is the most unusual of the cranes. Several subspecies of crowned cranes live in Africa, including the black-necked northern crowned crane of West Africa and the gray-necked southern and eastern varieties, which range from South Africa to the Equator. Crowned cranes subsist largely on seeds and insects. They often capture insects by stamping on the ground to dislodge them from their cover.

Whether performing a mating dance in Tanzania's Ngorongoro Crater (above) or feeding on the aquatic life of a marsh in Kenya (right), the eastern crowned crane is a regal presence whose likeness has been adopted as the national emblem of Uganda.

A slender bill provides the wattled crane (left) with a means of gathering a wide variety of foods. All day it patrols its feeding territory, digging in the soil with its bill and extracting tubers, roots and insects. Though it also eats grain crops, its numbers are too small to inflict serious damage.

African Cousins

Picking out a bustard among the cranes with which it shares its African range would not be difficult. But an observer might find it hard to believe that the bustard is a relative of its neighbors on the savanna. Bustards, like the Arabian bustard pictured at left with a carmine bee-eater on its back, are savanna-dwelling relatives of cranes. Among the family's 23 species are the heaviest flying land birds. One species, the great bustard of Europe, weighs up to 37 pounds. Generally nesting in open grasslands, bustards are omnivorous, feeding on grasses and plant parts, insects—especially grasshoppers—mice, lizards and other small animals.

A distant cousin of the bustard is the wattled crane (above, left), named for the white-feathered wattles hanging from its chin. Even more conspicuous are the red warts that cover the front of its face. Like the Stanley, or blue, crane (opposite), its habitat is exclusively African, and, like most other cranes, it is becoming increasingly rare.

The national bird of South Africa, the Stanley, or blue, crane, is pictured in its typical resting posture. Since Stanley cranes consume prodigious numbers of locusts, the birds have been of great service to man, particularly during those years when the insect's population has increased dramatically.

119

Indian Love Call

The sarus crane, which lives primarily in India but is also found in parts of Asia as far east as the Philippines, is a stately bird of considerable size, sometimes almost five feet tall. Sarus cranes are thought to mate for life, a partnership that is reaffirmed by frequent simultaneous trumpeting. These "unison calls" (left) take place with male and female standing at attention, bills pointed skyward, the male with his wings raised and displayed while the female holds hers closely to her sides. The bird sounds the call by blowing air through its unusual windpipe, which is convoluted inside the breastbone like the coils of a French horn. As a result, the sound is greatly amplified and may carry for more than two miles.

Sarus females generally produce a clutch of two eggs each year, usually in late summer, laying them in nests located in shallow marsh water. Both parents take turns incubating the eggs, rising now and then to turn them over to receive maximum warmth (below).

An adult sarus attends its newly hatched chicks in this unusual photograph, taken near Delhi, India. At hatching, the chick is a rust-colored ball of down—so weak that it is unable to leave the nest for a few days. When alerted by a call from a parent, the young freeze motionless in the nest until the adult sounds the "all clear." The chicks grow rapidly and soon are able to gather most of their own food, though they generally stay with their parents for at least 10 months.

Whooper Revival

Under careful management the whooping crane is slowly recovering from a population decline to an all-time low of 21 wild and captive birds in the early 1950s. A unique foster-parent program was undertaken by the U.S. and Canadian wildlife services in 1975 to guard against a repetition of the 1940 catastrophe in which a hurricane all but destroyed one of the two wild whooping crane flocks.

Scientists were aware that although a whooper generally lays a clutch of two eggs, competition for food usually allows only one young bird to reach maturity. In a Canadian program designed to insure the survival of both eggs, the second egg was removed from the whoopers' nests and transported to Idaho nesting sites of the sandhill cranes. Thanks to the sandhills, shown in flight (overleaf), wildlife experts have raised the whoopers' wild population by a minimum of 10 birds a year since the program's inception.

Engaged in a territorial dispute (left) or preparing for takeoff (below), the whooping crane is an elegant bird that has been at the center of controversy for years. While some environmentalists say the bird is doomed in its natural habitat and should be preserved only in captivity, others contend that whoopers should be nurtured in the wild in any way possible. Efforts such as the foster-parent program have raised the whooper population, wild and captive, to around 100 birds—a fivefold increase in 25 years.

Credits

Cover—G. Meszaros, Bruce Coleman, Inc. 1—Tom Brakefield. 5—J.&D. Bartlett, B.C. 6–7, 9—George Silk. 15—K.W. Fink, Photo Researchers. 16—G.R. Zahm, B.C. 16–17—Tom Brakefield. 18—George Silk. 19 (left)—K.W. Fink, P.R., (right)—M. Bruhmuller, Animals Animals. 20—R. Carr, B.C. 21—S. Bisserot, B.C. 22—W.H. Hudson, Animals Animals. 23—G. Holton, P.R. 25—Tom Brakefield. 26—L.R. Ditto, B.C. 27—H.S. Banton, P.R. 28–9—J.&D. Bartlett, B.C. 29—L.L. Rue III, B.C. 30—L. McIntyre, Animals Animals. 31—Co Rentmeester. 33—J.&D. Bartlett, B.C. 34—T. McHugh, P.R. 35 (top)—S. Krasemann, P.R., (bottom)—H. Engels, B.C. 36–7—T. McHugh, P.R. 38—A. Mercieca, P.R., 39—Tom Brakefield. 40—C. Ott, P.R. 41—George Silk. 42—J. Dominis, Time Inc. 43—C. Ott, P.R. 46 (left)—R. Bloomfield, B.C., (right)—T. McHugh, P.R. 47—C. Frith, B.C. 48–9—George Silk. 50—G. Schaller, B.C. 51—F. Alsop III, B.C. 52—Peter B. Kaplan. 53—J. Borneman, P.R. 54—N. Myers, B.C. 55—Peter B. Kaplan. 57—R. Austing, B.C. 58—D.&R. Sullivan, B.C. 59 (left)—G. Plage, B.C., (right)—R. Carr, B.C. 60 (left)—K.W. Fink, B.C. 60–1—George Silk. 61 (top, right)—N. Fox-Davies, (bottom)—M. Fogden, B.C. 62—Durden, B.C. 63 (top)—J. Markham, B.C., (bottom)—P. Hinchliffe, B.C. 64—George Silk. 65 (top)—G. Zahm, B.C., (bottom)—R. Carr, B.C. 67—J. Dominis, Time Inc. 68 (top)—A. Mercieca, P.R., (bottom)—B.&C. Calhoun, B.C. 69—W. Harvey, P.R. 70 (top)—J. Hoffman, B.C., (bottom)—P. Schwartz, P.R. 71—O.S. Pettingill, P.R. 73 (top, left)—R. Kinne, P.R., (top, right)—K.W. Fink, B.C., (bottom, left)—G. Harrison, B.C., (bottom, right)—Peter B. Kaplan. 74–5—Kessel, Time Inc. 75—Wolfgang Bayer. 76—T. McHugh, P.R. 77 (top, left), (bottom, left)—G. Holton, P.R., (right)—F. Erize, B.C. 78—J. Dominis, Time Inc. 79—E. Hosking, B.C. 80–1—M.P. Kahl, B.C. 84—G. Holton, P.R.

84–5—T. McHugh, P.R. 87—George Silk. 88 (left)—C. Haagner, B.C., (right)—S. Dalton, P.R. 89 (top, left)—T. McHugh, Healesville Sanctuary, P.R., (top, right)—R. Kinne, P.R., (bottom, left)—M. Castro, P.R., (bottom, right)—Bruce Coleman, Inc. 90—L. West, B.C. 91—G. Zahm, B.C. 99—L. Stone, P.R. 100 (left)—S. Dalton, P.R., (right)—Van Nostrand, P.R. 101 (left)—Thase Daniel, (right)—R. Kinne, P.R. 102—G.D. Plage, B.C. 103 (top)—R. Kinne, P.R., (bottom)—M.&R. Borland, B.C. 104—J. Fields, P.R. 105 (top, right)—A.W. Ambler, P.R., (center, right)—R. Parker, P.R., (bottom, right)—G. Harrison, B.C. 106, 107—C.B. Frith, B.C. 109—D.&R. Sullivan, B.C. 110 (left)—S. Dalton, P.R., (right)—J. Markham, B.C. 111—Oxford Scientific Films, B.C. 112—Panuska, DPI. 113 (bottom)—F. Grehan. 115—R.E. Pelham, B.C. 116—K. Tweedy-Holmes, Animals Animals. 116–7—J.S. Flannery, B.C. 118 (top)—T. McHugh for Bronx Zoo, P.R., (bottom)—L. Lyon, B.C. 119—T. McHugh, P.R. 120, 121—M.P. Kahl, B.C. 122—M. Stouffer, Nat'l. Audubon Society Col., P.R. 123—R. Kinne, P.R. 124–5—G. Zahm, B.C.

Photographs on endpapers are used courtesy of Time-Life Picture Agency, Russ Kinne and Stephen Dalton of Photo Researchers, Inc. and Nina Leen.

Film sequences on pages 8 and 13 are from "Kodiak Island" and "Owls," programs in the Time-Life Television series *Wild, Wild World of Animals*.

ILLUSTRATION on pp. 10–11 by Paul Singer, those on p. 12 by Enid Kotschnig, those on 44, 45 courtesy Bettmann Archive, the drawing on p. 82 is by James Thurber, those on pages 92–97 are by John Groth. The illustration on page 113 (top) is by Roger Tory Peterson, courtesy of Mill Pond Press.

Bibliography

NOTE: Asterisk at the left means that a paperback volume is also listed in *Books in Print*.

Austin, Oliver Jr., *Birds of the World*. Golden Press, 1961.

Beebe, William, *Pheasants: Their Lives and Homes*. Doubleday, 1926.

*Bent, A. C., *Life Histories of North American Birds of Prey*. Dover Publications, 1958.

*———, *Life Histories of North American Woodpeckers*. Dover Publications, 1964.

Brown, L., and Amadon, D., *Eagles, Hawks and Falcons of the World*. McGraw-Hill, 1968.

Bruun, Bertel, *British and European Birds in Color*. Paul Hamlyn, 1969.

Burton, J. A., ed., *Owls of the World, Their Evolution, Structure and Ecology*. E. P. Dutton, 1973.

Delacour, Jean, *The Pheasants of the World*. Charles Scribner's Sons, 1951.

———, and Amadon, D., *Curassows and Related Birds*. American Museum of Natural History, 1973.

Dorst, Jean, *The Life of Birds*. Columbia University Press, 1974.

Ford, Alice, ed., *The Bird Biographies of John James Audubon*. The Macmillan Company, 1957.

Forshaw, J. H., *Parrots of the World*. Doubleday, 1973.

Gilliard, W. Thomas, *Living Birds of the World*. Doubleday, 1958.

Greenewalt, C. H., *Hummingbirds*. Doubleday, 1960.

———, "Marvelous Hummingbird." *National Geographic*, July, 1966, pp. 98–101.

Greenway, J. C., Jr., *Extinct and Vanishing Birds of the World*. American Committee for International Wildlife Protection, 1958.

Grimmer, J. L., "Strange Little World of the Hoatzin." *National Geographic*, September, 1962, pp. 391–400.

Grossman, Mary L., and Hamlet, J., *Birds of Prey of the World*. Potter, 1970.

Grzimek, Bernhard, *Grzimek's Animal Life Encyclopedia*, Vols. 8, 9, 10. Van Nostrand Reinhold, 1973.

Johnsgard, Paul A., *Grouse and Quails of North America*. University of Nebraska Press, 1973.

Krutch, Joseph Wood, and Erikkson, Paul S., *A Treasury of Bird Lore*. Paul Erikkson, 1962.

McNulty, Faith, *The Whooping Crane*. E. P. Dutton, 1966.

Murphy, R. C., and Amadon, D., *Land Birds of America*. McGraw-Hill, 1953.

Ogburn, Charlton, *The Adventure of Birds*. William Morrow, 1976.

Peterson, Roger Tory, *The Bird Watcher's Anthology*. Harcourt, Brace, 1957.

———, and the editors of Time-Life Books. *The Birds*. Time-Life, 1969.

Root, J., and Root, A., "Inside a Hornbill's Walled-up Nest." *National Geographic*, December, 1969, pp. 846–856.

Scheithauer, W., *Hummingbirds*. Thomas Y. Crowell, 1966.

Skutch, A. F., *The Life of the Hummingbird*. Crown, 1973.

Thomson, A. Lansborough, ed., *A New Dictionary of Birds*. McGraw-Hill, 1964.

Truslow, F. K., "Eye to Eye With Eagles in the Everglades." *National Geographic*, January, 1961, pp. 123–147.

Van Lawick-Goodall, Jane, "Tool-using Bird: The Egyptian Vulture." *National Geographic*, May, 1968, pp. 631–641.

Walkenshaw, L. H., *Cranes of the World*. Winchester Press, 1973.

Wetmore, Alexander, *Water, Prey and Game Birds of North America*. National Geographic Book Service, 1964.

Index